WOMEN'S VENTURES

VENTURES

women's visions

29 inspiring stories from women who started their own businesses

by Shoshana Alexander

THE CROSSING PRESS
FREEDOM, CALIFORNIA

Photo Credits

Lynn Winter, pages 11, 12, 15 by John Nation
Barbara Hughley, pages 20, 21, 23 by Media Professionals
Laurel Burch, pages 27, 28 by Rick Sara, p. 31 by Steve Fukuda
Ann Ruethling, pages 43, 44, by ©Debra Lex Photography
Barbara Beckmann, pages 55, 56 by Errol Novickas
Polly Helm, pages 61, 62 by Paul Carter, page 65 courtesy of University of Oregon Knight
    Library Special Collections
Theresa Martinez Hoffacker, pages 77, 78, 81 ©Linda Montoya
Marcy Carsey, pages 84, 85 by courtesy of Carsey-Werner
Sarahn Henderson, pages 125, 126, 129 by Sally Holst-Crooks
Gayle McEnroe, pages 139, 140, 142 ©Doug Beasley, Doug Beasley Photo Inc.
Tami Simon, pages 146, 147, 149 by Steven Collector
Jenai Lane, pages 153, 154, 156 by Dave Casteel
Sylvia Warren, pages 193, 194 by Shoshana Alexander
Shoshana Alexander, back cover by Larry Marcus

We would also like to thank all of the other contributing photographers and the people who helped collect the photographs for the book.

Library of Congress Cataloging-in-Publication Data
Alexander, Shoshana
    Women's Ventures, women's visions : 29 inspiring stories from women who started their own business / by Shoshana Alexander.
        p.   cm.
    ISBN 0-89594-823-0 (pbk.)
    1. Businesswomen--United States--Case studies. 2. Self-employed women--United States--Case studies. 3. Women-owned business enterprises--United States--Case studies. 4. Entrepreneurship--United States--Case studies. 4. Entrepreneurship--United States--Case studies. I. Title.
HD6072.6.U5A44   1997
658.4'21'082--dc21   97-22531
                                                                                                           CIP

ACKNOWLEDGMENTS

Many contributed time and spirit to make this book a reality. Elaine Gill and Karen Narita of The Crossing Press conceived the idea and set the book in motion. I am deeply grateful to my editor and friend, Linda Gunnarson, whose genuine interest and enthusiasm for inspiring women to find their true Work helped to conceptualize the material and guide it to completion. Thanks to Patti Trimble, poet, artist, and friend, for inspiring a decent title for this book. And to Jane Lazear for carrying it on. Thanks to Cyndi Barnes, Production Manager, for her understanding help.

The women featured here generously made time in the midst of intense schedules to tell me their stories and work interactively to complete them. May the unique and powerful voice of each ring out from their words. During the course of the interviews, I felt as if I were convening a wonderful gathering of women who together were creating a light to guide and encourage all those who long to fulfill a vision or a dream.

Thanks to the many friends, acquaintances, organizations, authors, and women business-owners who guided me to numerous magnificent candidates. Among those who helped are: Rick and Gair Crutcher, Barbara Austin, Susan Tieger, Joline Godfrey, Sypko

Andreae, Carolyn Shaffer, Peter Werner, Patricia Atkins, Terry Herkimer at the Center for Independent Living in Berkeley, Joan Bergman, Elena Featherston, Phyllis Apelbaum, Dan Drasin, Lynn Lori Sylvan and Adetola, Barbara Gates, Leticia Wiley, Aviva Jill Romm, Linda Gunnerson and staff at The Crossing Press, Carly Newfeld, Suzanne Arms, Justine Toms, Carol Berry, Laura Ledesma, the National Association for Women in Construction, Women's Initiative for Self-Employment (WISE) in San Francisco, Eric Utne, Penny Rosenwasser, Elaine Meisch, Linda Haithcox at the NAACP headquarters in Baltimore, Kris Welch, NAJDA, and others along the way who gave their time. A special thanks to Helen Waite of Eagle's Nest Camp and Pam Johnson of the Nashville Cat Care Center for their work and their stories. I spoke with many others or received moving communications from wonderful women business owners who are not included here but whose inspiring work places them among those gathered.

A special thanks to Studs Terkel for pioneering a genre to celebrate the human voice and spirit in all its variations that helped to inspire the style of this book. Thanks to Nancy Goddard for coaching that set the energy in motion. As always, gratitude to Ted and Laurinda and to Sypko and Carolyn for being "family." Jim Wiley gave the gift of time to work. Nancy Bloom and her "ghost-writers in the sky" made completion possible. Michael Dennison generously offered eleventh-hour insights and the perfect phrase. Special gratitude to my mother Carol Berry for willing and effective research on a moment's notice. Continuing and endless thanks to Sypko Andreae, Angel of Communications Technologies and true friend, for his foresight and magnanimity in so many ways, including dedicated godfathering. Thanks to the trees. And my deepest appreciation to my son Elias Alexander for, once again, sharing his mother with a book.

CONTENTS

INTRODUCTION

For a woman, starting a business has as much to do with who she has been and wants to be as it does with the products and services she offers. It invariably means taking a road with steep hills and harrowing turns into the unknown. Meeting the challenge brings the exhilarating rewards of finding herself empowered in a venture uniquely her own and engaged in what so many in this book describe as "doing what I was meant to do." Impassioned by an idea or gripped by a calling, the women who tell their stories here moved forward with courage and perseverance, building their bridges before them. To encourage others to fulfill their own dreams and visions, these remarkable women recount what led them to start their own businesses and how they launched them.

These profiles, based primarily on personal conversations, are not a representative sampling of *types* of businesses but rather a sampling of the *spirit* that sets a woman on the road to her own business. The women who speak here reflect the tremendous diversity in age, socio-economic class, geographical location, and ethnic background of women business-owners in the United States today. One out of every three businesses is currently owned by a woman—nearly eight million nationwide.* In less than a century, women have moved from lacking the right to vote to being a power that is transforming our entire culture through economic leverage and innovative business practices. It is estimated that after the turn of the century, forty to fifty percent of all businesses will be owned by women.

While there are many ways in which women come to business-ownership, those included here started with their own ideas. Some came to business fully prepared; others didn't know the first thing about it. For some, starting a business was a direct goal, while for others a business happened to unfold as they did what they loved to do. Some assiduously followed the steps of a business plan while others felt their way from tree to tree. By whatever avenue they arrived, creating a business was a process that arose out of the entirety of their lives.

Although each has a unique story, there are several common threads. Every woman who speaks here reached a turning point that required her to choose a new direction. For some it was because they were turning 30 . . . or 40 . . . or 50, because a door opened and they were ready to walk through, or because a door closed and they had to go on. These are women who lost a job or could no longer in conscience remain in one. They are women who were stopped at the glass ceiling, or who realized that what went on beyond that invisible barrier was not worth their time and energy. They are women whose love for their children transformed their careers.

---

* It must be noted that this figure may be an overcount, since any business in which 50% or more of the owners are women is classified by the Census Bureau as "woman-owned." When both spouses equally own a business, for example, ownership is assigned to the woman. An unfortunate side-effect of this practice is that in order to take advantage of government equal-opportunity programs, women are sometimes installed as titular heads of businesses that are actually male-owned and run.

Some, knowing that something in their lives had to change although not sure what or how, went traveling or sought silence. In this time outside of time, a new direction could emerge. Some deliberated for years while others were compelled by circumstances to leap into a new life. Whether pulled by a vision or urged on by necessity, they chose to move forward, trusting the glimmer of an idea or an irresistible prompting.

Starting a business is challenging for any entrepreneur, but for a woman the challenges can be amplified. As she crosses the threshold into an arena where she takes an active part in formulating the rules, she is often challenged to prove herself. She may be discounted, disbelieved, or devalued in the marketplace and at the negotiating table simply because she is a woman. This is not to deny that many women have been valued and encouraged by men who are spouses, investors, friends and coworkers. But faceless sexism persists.

For women of color, establishing a business amidst the structures of racism adds another obstacle to the course. As a consultant for small businesses, Sylvia Warren has noted that "people would talk to me on the phone and make an appointment, but when they arrived in the lobby and found an African-American woman, I could see in their faces that moment of surprise . . . and a host of other responses. For men especially, I think it can be disconcerting that I am offering a particular kind of expertise which in this society is not attributed to African Americans in general and not to women in particular, at least not to women of color." In overcoming such obstacles the triumph is great.

The biggest challenge any business faces is finding capital and establishing credit. For women this challenge too is magnified. Despite their record of lower delinquency on loans, women have generally found it harder than men to secure credit. Jenai Lane of

Respect was literally laughed at when she applied for a bank loan. Determined and resourceful, we see the women in this book, like millions of others, starting their businesses on a few thousand dollars or finding alternative sources of funding. Susan Levy of Femi-9 Contracting Corporation had a small settlement from an automobile accident that she used as start-up capital. Tami Simon of Sounds True Catalog received a modest inheritance from her father.

For many others acquiring capital meant asking for loans from family and friends, or drawing upon personal savings. Some used credit cards. Access to capital for women business owners has improved only in the last few years. "Bankers have begun to recognize that the nearly 8 million women-owned businesses in this country are a great, untapped market," reports Susan Peterson, Chair of the National Foundation for Women Business Owners (NFWBO). "The challenges faced by women entrepreneurs have not disappeared, however," she adds. "Women business owners still have lower levels of available credit than their male counterparts."

Despite the challenges, women in the U.S. continue to launch businesses at twice the rate of men, and they are substantially changing how business is done. In a lawsuit in federal court, Belinda Guadarrama of GCMicro challenged the federal government to comply with its own guidelines for distributing contracts to minority-owned businesses; winning her case in court meant hundreds of millions of dollars worth of contracts for small businesses owned by minorities. In face of misdirected city ordinances which impeded her opening a therapeutic massage center, Sister Rosalind Gefre, member of a Catholic religious order, worked with her city council to help rewrite the laws.

In creating their own businesses, women are altering internal restrictions as well as external ones. In the corporate world, for instance, age may limit opportunities; in the world of small business, teens and grandmothers are creating their own companies. While the majority of women business owners in the U.S. are between 25 and 54 years of age, more than 8 percent are over 65.

Women are bringing into the business world values that place them in the forefront of a major and pervasive cultural shift. Integrity, cooperation, intuition, service, win-win strategies, encouragement, and mutual support are qualities that many women offer their employees and clients, and these are proving to be solid and successful business practices. Sally Helgesen, author of *The Female Advantage* and *The Web of Inclusion*, noted that in their successful businesses "women tended to put themselves at the centers of their organizations rather than at the top, thus emphasizing both accessibility and equality, and…they labored constantly to include people in their decision-making. This had the effect of undermining the boundaries so characteristic of mainstream organizations, with their strict job descriptions, categorizing of people according to rank and their restrictions on the flow of information."

In founding and sustaining their businesses, the quality of their relationships has been vital to the women in this book. Joline Godfrey, author of *Our Wildest Dreams: Women Entrepreneurs Making Money, Having Fun, Doing Good*, points out that "Women who own businesses often express as much pleasure in the relationships required to make the business work as with excellence, increased profits, and growth in self-esteem." As the women here reveal, they tend to regard their employees as personal relationships, sometimes even friends, rather than as assets and resources. Gayle McEnroe of Metal Services Inc. puts it, "When I look at employees, I see not only them but also their spouses and children and how they all depend upon every move of the company. They depend upon me doing the right thing and using good judgment. They depend upon the company being a good steward of whatever prosperity we receive." Perhaps it is this ability to consider the entirety of a human life that accounts for the fact that "women-owned businesses are more likely to offer flex-time, childcare, and other 'family-friendly' practices than U.S. businesses generally."*

Valuing family and relationship and giving it priority has in fact determined the course of business for several of these women. Barbara Hughley left her executive position at a Madison Avenue advertising agency when her daughter Kristelle needed urgent care and later located the offices of her own business two minutes away from her daughter's school. Theresa Martinez Hoffacker's child-care center provided a place where she could work and also care for her own children. Patrice Harrison-Inglis's hobby of making goat cheese turned into a family business that now includes her two boys as well as her husband. A number of women profiled here now employ their husbands or have made them partners in their business. "We loved each other and wanted to work together," Patrice Wynne of GAIA Bookstore and Community Center candidly explains her decision to share ownership and management of her business with her husband, Eric Joost.

A number of women in this book also found that their tendency to care deeply about relationships is one of their greatest challenges as business owners. "For a long time all of the employer-employee relationships were very blurry for me," comments Tami Simon of Sounds True Catalog. "Now I have gotten clear that my

* From "Expanding Business Opportunities for Women: The 1995 Report of the Interagency Committee on Women's Business Enterprise." Published in cooperation with the National Women's Business Council, January 1996, p. 4.

friends are my friends, and my employees are my employees. It doesn't mean that there's not a lot of love and affection in the employee-employer relationship—because there is. If you walked through our offices, you'd feel tremendous love between me and a lot of people who work here. But I'm not there emotionally for them in the same way that I am for my friends. These are working relationships that are defined by a different set of parameters. It's complicated though, and I'm still learning a lot about it."

This attitude of genuine caring can become especially difficult for women employers when it comes to performance expectations. "I tend to see who a person wants to become rather than the reality of who they are and how they fit into the business," says Patrice Wynne. "When problems emerge with an employee, I end up sticking them under my great big wing and spending inordinate amounts of time and energy trying to bring them along at my own expense. It's a huge problem for women in business that a man in a similar situation wouldn't encounter. While a man might say, 'It's not working. You're out of here,' I tend to say, 'She really means well. She didn't mean to do it. If I give her that work to do, it will put her over the edge. I'll just do it myself.'" Patrice recently hired an executive coach who encourages and supports her in "asking for what I need to move the business forward." Many report that it has taken a great deal of experimentation to sort out the rules for the woman-run, post-industrial workplace where employees are seen as human beings rather than cogs in a machine.

The qualities these women are bringing to their businesses spill over into the choices they make for their communities as well. Financial self-sufficiency and independence provide the opportunity to foster interdependence. Newspaper publisher Assunta Ng declares, "As long as I run a business, I will use every opportunity to make sure that we develop New Girls' Networks in every format and in every segment of the society, so that women helping other women in business is just something that we accept as part of our daily lives."

For virtually all of the women in this book, the ability to be of service to their communities goes hand in hand to some degree with being a business-owner. For Gayle McEnroe, "The biggest thrill in business is being in a position to extend opportunity to other people, because it has certainly been extended to me." Barbara Hughley felt the same. Before she left her position as vice-president with a major advertising firm, she had more African-Americans on staff than any other advertising agency on Madison Avenue. "I went out to Howard University to recruit, or I promoted young black men and women who showed a lot of potential." For Nabila Mango, owning a small computer export firm allows her the flexibility to devote time to teaching and promoting Arabic culture and heritage. Jenai Lane of Respect reports that "This last year I got to write checks for pretty substantial amounts of money to over ten organizations, and that felt so good to do. My favorite thing to do is to give money to organizations I support."

Whether as owners of multi-million dollar companies or as heads of homebased enterprises, the women in this book revel in their capacity to bring in money and to choose how to redistribute it. Yet their definition of success has as much to do with the fulfillment they experience in their daily lives as it does with their spreadsheets. In fact, NFWBO reports that, in a survey of women on the rewards of business ownership, ranking higher than financial rewards were control and independence, the satisfaction of growing a business, helping people, recognition, and building relationships.

For the women who tell their stories here, creating a business has meant holding a vision of possibility and making it real, seeing a need and filling it, hearing a call and answering it. For them, starting a business has arisen from knowing there is a better way and setting out to create it. Establishing their enterprises has been the result of both good ideas and inspiration, of sound judgment and of miracles. For each woman here, starting her own business has meant the triumph and pleasure of doing what only she can do.

The women in this book are perhaps not that different from any of us who have an idea for an endeavor that can bring personal and financial satisfaction and give us the opportunity to make a contribution. What distinguishes them is that they have done it. Here, in voices grateful, proud, joyful and sure, they tell us how.

Shoshana Alexander

LYNN WINTER

Lynn's Paradise Cafe
Louisville, Kentucky

Lynn's Paradise Cafe, which opened in 1991, offers downhome food border-

ing on gourmet in an atmosphere that has, as Lynn describes it, "an eclectic

esthetic." Outside, an 8-foot high, red coffee pot fountain pours coffee into a

mammoth concrete cup. Customers readily wait in line—treated to free

coffee and, for those with children, a special play area with vintage toys.

The menu, designed by Lynn and one of the waitresses, won a National

Restaurant Association award in 1994, and the restaurant has been named

one of The Best of Louisville. Owner Lynn Winter manages 85 employees,

and still cooks, waits tables, and generally keeps whimsy in the atmosphere.

Certain restaurants have a sense of "home"—that feeling of food and people—that grips me down in my soul. The Homestyle Cafe in northern California was a place like that, very quirky and casual, where fishermen and loggers came to eat. It was one of my favorite places. I had moved to the area from Kentucky in the early '80s to study with a master furniture maker from Sweden whose vision and craftsmanship seemed almost spiritual to me. I was a woodworker, and I eventually set up my own business, making one-of-a-kind pieces at my little shop in a converted water tower in the artsy coastal town of Mendocino.

One Sunday morning, my sweetheart and I were eating breakfast at the Homestyle. The place was completely packed that day. Suddenly the owner of the place appeared at my table and said, "Oh, my God. Do you know how to wait tables?" I said "Well . . . yes." She handed me her order book and said, "I'm having an asthma attack. Take over." I had been working in restaurants off and on since I was 15, so I knew what to do—but I don't know how she knew that. I jumped up, put on her apron, and went to work. I *loved* waiting tables. I always had. Whenever I waited tables, it felt like I was doing absolutely the right thing.

The next day I went back and got a part-time job there. At first it was just for fun—I was a woodworker putting in a little time as a waitress. But after a year at the Homestyle, I decided I didn't want to do woodworking anymore. I was good at it, but I didn't love it in the way I loved waiting tables. I just loved serving people, the relationships that develop, and the kind of things you can do. There was something so intrinsically good for me in that.

So I sold my entire business—years' worth of wood that I had collected and most of my equipment—without even knowing what I was going toward. I thought, "Life is too short not to do what you love." Everyone else thought I was absolutely crazy.

A year later a dear friend suggested that I start my own restaurant. I must have been ready to hear it, because I felt like a bolt of lightning had hit me. Everything in me absolutely recognized that's what I wanted to do. It was an epiphany. I had found my path. Starting my own restaurant was what I was meant to do with my life.

From that day on, I did everything in my power to make that realization come true. I continued at the Homestyle, but I knew that if I wanted my own restaurant, I'd have to get experience in other kinds of restaurants as well. There was a place in town called the Cafe Beaujolais that was on the cutting edge of the new California cuisine. I'd never eaten there, but I knew its reputation. Instinctively I knew I wanted to work there, but I felt too intimidated to go in. I was feeding fishermen and loggers in this funky little cafe on the coast; I was not the material a French nouvelle cuisine restaurant would be looking for.

Yet I knew I had to move on. I gave my two weeks notice at the Homestyle and quit without having another job in hand. When my last day was over, I was sitting at home in my little kitchen when the phone rang. It was the manager at the Beaujolais. She said, "We hear you're looking for a job. Would you like to come down and apply?" "How in the world did you ever get my name?" I asked her. "I don't really know," she said.

The next four years, working at the Beaujolais, I soaked up everything I could. I worked a lot, and I learned a lot. When they needed to hire someone to cook, I grabbed the chance, taking on extra shifts to do it. All during that time, I kept thinking about how I was going to decorate my own restaurant, what my own style was, etc. Whenever I had a day off, I would travel to flea markets to buy things for my future restaurant. I ate out whenever I wasn't working—sometimes I'd eat at six different places in a day—to see what worked and what didn't work. I was completely focused on my dream.

I knew it would happen, although I didn't know how or where. But I never considered moving back to Kentucky. In the midst of this process, my parents came out to visit. My dad and I went for a walk and he told me that he had prostate cancer and wanted me to be home for the operation. I told him my dream of having a restaurant. He is a businessman, and the way he likes to remember the story is: "She told me she wanted to go to the College of the Redwoods to learn how to go into business, and I told her the only way to learn business is to do it." He told me that if I moved back home, they could help me. He and I were so much alike that for years we had been constantly at loggerheads. I wasn't sure. . . .

I went home for his operation, which was successful, and it was like life was given back to our whole family. On his first day back from the hospital, I got a call from a local friend of mine who knew about my idea. "Lynn, there's a restaurant going out of business. You ought to go down and look at the place." I said to my dad that, if he didn't mind, I'd like to slip out to see it. He said, "Damn, I'm going with you too!" He got into the car in his bathrobe and with

his catheter, and we drove down there together. It turned out to be a terrible location, but for me the event was pivotal. His brush with death and my determination put us on the same side. My folks were willing to help me have my own restaurant—and I was now willing to move back to Kentucky.

They gave me their retirement money to get started—barely enough, but that's what I had and I had to make it work. Those first two years of starting the restaurant I call "the hell years." I had to look for real estate, buy equipment, create my menu, do my own advertising and hiring, handle all the taxes, develop all the systems. The cheapest way to get equipment was to buy it used at auctions. I'd arrive with my tool belt on to look over a piece of equipment; I'd take it apart, try to figure it out—all the while I didn't know what the heck I was doing. There were no other women out there doing this. I'd ask these big burly guys, "Excuse me, can you tell me what makes a good gas stove?" I had my dad's pick-up truck, and I'd have to beg these guys to help me load all this stuff. It was a pretty solitary journey at that point.

At one auction, I stood for thirteen hours on a concrete floor in a building with no heat in the winter, just so I could get some chairs that I wanted. By the time they came up, everybody there must have taken pity on me because nobody bargained against me. I got them for two or three dollars a piece, and I still have them. Meanwhile, I was storing all this stuff in my parents' garage.

The first six months were a very harrowing time. I was desperate, because I couldn't find a location—and I *needed* to be in business. On my twenty-ninth birthday, an equipment salesman I knew took me to see a restaurant in Louisville that was going out of business—it turned out that it wasn't the equipment he wanted me to see, but the place itself. *That* was the building I was looking for! It would need to be completely gutted, but I just had to make it work.

The minute I found this building, I became the general contractor. I had to learn how to do everything—fast and cheap. I worked from four o'clock in the morning to midnight every day. I couldn't afford to rent a place to live so I just put down a sleeping bag there at night. Every morning 20 to 25 guys arrived, and I worked alongside them, learning how to do demolition, plumbing, electrical work, gas lines. I designed the place, drawing the blueprints for the floorplan on a piece of graph paper. I did dry wall, pipe fitting, carpet laying—me, who had never really even helped around the house much! The challenges were incredible. Not only putting in the restaurant, but getting all the *permits* as well. My dad was having his doubts about whether they would ever see their $60,000 again. When I brought my mother down to see the building, I was so excited—I had finally found a location. She took a look around, walked up the stairs, and burst into tears of dismay.

It was like being a fish fighting upstream constantly. But I had no choice, there was no going back. This was my dream. I could see what could be, even when nobody else could see it.

Two and a half months after I had signed the lease on that building, we opened for business. It was an unbelievable situation. I had hired eleven people because I liked them and knew I could work with them, but none of them had ever worked in a restaurant before. We had almost no idea what we were doing. We didn't even have table numbers.

One customer who I thought was just great started coming in as a regular. She was very funny, and I loved talking with her when I was waiting tables. One day I filled her coffee cup, then crossed the room to greet another person I'd been getting to know through my boyfriend. Indicating the woman I'd just spoken with, he said in a hushed voice, "You know who that is, don't you?" I said, "No, who?" "That's the food critic for the Courier Journal." I strode back to her table and said, "I'm going to kill you if you're the food critic! I was really starting to like you. I can't believe it! Now we can't be friends."

We had been open less than a month. About a week later, the paper called us to say the review would be coming out the next day, a Saturday. They wouldn't tell me if it was good, bad or indifferent. But we stayed up all night cooking, to be prepared. The review was great, and despite the fact that the irreplaceable cook I had personally prepared for one major position never showed up, we pulled it off. The review packed us, and ever since then we have kept getting busier and busier. And our first reviewer, who is no longer the food critic, has become one of my best friends.

People come to the Paradise Cafe not only because the food is good, but because of what the place does to them. I really believe in stretching creativity and doing wild things—projects that people would otherwise never do—like the concrete farm animals outside, and the 8-foot high coffee pot. In the fall we carve 120 pumpkins in the restaurant, and you see adults sitting on the floor in the midst of this gigantic mess. We hold an annual Easter Egg Decorating Contest, and the winner gets free breakfast for a month without any wait. In the spring we get people blowing out eggs and decorating them to hang on trees inside the restaurant. We have toys on every table—banana noses and pop guns that shoot bits of raw potato.

I feel that the things people use in their daily lives should be fun and beautiful. That's why I was a woodworker. That's why we have beautiful antique salt and pepper shakers on every table and funny cracker holders and toys. In the beginning people said to me,

"They're gonna steal you blind," and I said, "Well, if they do, I'll just replace the things." I tell you, instead a day hasn't gone by when I haven't found something new that a customer has left on the table for us.

People come to my place because they feel creative here, they feel alive, they get a chance to be zany without judgment. I've built my business on that.

BARBARA HUGHLEY

Media Professionals, Inc.
Baldwin, New York

Barbara Hughley was a senior vice president at Ogilvy & Mather, one of Madison Avenue's top advertising agencies, when her concern for her daughter's health took priority over her career. The choice to leave her job led her to eventually start her own advertising business. Her clients now include Don Cornelius Productions, The Essence Awards and the National Association of Black McDonald's Owners and Operators. Recipient of many awards, Barbara is also the first African-American woman to own a radio station in New York. She is currently Chair of the Minority Workshop for the International Radio and Television Society, the same organization that 24 years earlier gave her her start in advertising.

I was getting ready for work one morning when an announcement on the radio caught my attention. It was about a program to introduce minorities to the advertising world. I took down the number and called to schedule an interview. I knew this was going to change my life. It had to. I was working at Tiffany's in Manhattan, living in a studio apartment in Queens with my two little children, and my ex-husband had recently remarried. Clearly, he and I were not going to be parenting as a team, working together to give our kids a good life. I would be able to get by on my income and child support—but that wasn't enough. I wanted *more* for my children, *a lot more!*

After my divorce I had worked my way through school, figuring that with a degree as a laboratory technician, I could get a job in a hospital and move up from there. My marriage had been spent supporting my husband through his education, but the marriage hadn't lasted long enough for me to get my turn. I was going through a pretty hard time emotionally as well as financially. I kept feeling sorry for myself, asking "Why me?" One day I got up and said to myself, "Just stop this now! Just go out there and pull it together." As soon as I did that, things began to come together. I started paying more attention to what was going on around me, and that's when I heard that radio ad.

When I went to the training interview, I was in the right mind-set to make it work. I wasn't just looking for a job, I was looking for an entire lifestyle change. Not getting accepted just wasn't an option. I got across to them that they wouldn't be sorry they selected me. Out of 300 applicants, I was one of 30 chosen to be trained for an entry level position in the media department of an advertising agency. I loved the field immediately. I knew this was my career path, and I was determined to take it as far as anyone could go. No one was going to stop me. I had to put my kids through college! At the end of the training, there were sixteen job positions available. I selected three to interview for and was offered all three. I chose Ogilvy & Mather because I would be assigned to work directly with the supervisor and the New York market buyer.

I entered as an assistant in the buying department. I worked with women there who used their paychecks to go across the street to Saks Fifth Avenue and buy silk blouses. I had a different agenda— I was trying to buy groceries. Six months after I started, I was promoted to the position of buyer. Every time I got a promotion, I asked what I had to do to get to the next level, then I would do that, and more. If I didn't get my promotion, I would ask why not. I held everybody accountable. After fourteen years and several promotions, I became a senior vice president, running the local broad-casting operation for six offices around the country, with 110 employees and an advertising budget of $300 million. My clients included many major names—Campbell Soup Company, American Express, AT&T, Kraft, General Foods.

By this time I had remarried and had another daughter. I was a wife, a mother and an executive, traveling about 65% of my work

time. I would do one-day trips to Houston from New York, so I could be home at night with my family, or I'd do an overnight in Los Angeles and be back in New York the next afternoon. Sometimes I'd wake up and not even know what city I was in. But I couldn't stop. I was obsessed with being the best. I had to win. And I did. I was named one of the 1986 Media All Stars by a national publication. In 1988 I was inducted into the Academy of Women Achievers. My clients loved working with me, and I always went the extra mile for them. I was always afraid that if I didn't slow down, one day I would explode, but I was too deep in it to stop. I needed to prove continuously that no one made a mistake by giving me the opportunity to succeed.

In 1990 I was sitting at Ogilvy & Mather with a bigger position than I had even imagined. Then I got a call from school saying that it looked like my ten-year-old daughter Kristelle had hurt her knees quite badly. When I took her to the doctor, he said, "I don't like what I see. You'll need to take her for some tests." The result was that she needed immediate surgery on both hips. She had a disorder that had been developing since birth; it would require two operations and about two years to get back on her feet.

My daughter was devastated! There was no question about what I had to do. I would get her through, no matter what it took. I resigned from my position. It turned my life upside down, but I thought, "If you can't be there for your daughter, what are you doing?" The first three months, we were in the hospital 24 hours a day, and I thought about nothing else. It was after she got home from the first surgery that I started getting scared, thinking, "Oh, my goodness, what am I going to do?" A large portion of the income coming into the house had been from my job. We still needed to do physical therapy for months, so I couldn't go back to the situation where I was working and traveling all the time. I had invested some of the capital from the sale of my Ogilvy & Mather stock into a start-up radio station. I knew, however, it would be years before I would see a return on that investment. Our nest egg was enough to last that first year, but then I'd have to figure out something. The one thing I still had was an excellent reputation—people kept calling to say, "Whenever you're ready to work, call."

When Kristelle started schoolwork with a tutor, I used the free time to contemplate my next move. Did I want to go back to work in the corporate world? It was very comfortable to get that paycheck every week and to have that level of recognition. I knew, however, if I went back, I would stay until I retired. This was my one chance to go out on my own and start my own business. What was the worst thing that could happen? I could always turn around and get a job.

I knew myself well enough to know that, instead of working out of my home, I needed to get out and have a real office and a secretary. For that, I needed start-up money. When I got a call about someone interested in investing in a media company, I went the investment route. In hindsight, it would have been a smarter financial move to get a loan through the Small Business Administration, but it actually never occurred to me that I might be qualified. Only later, when I applied for an expansion loan, did I learn that a start-up loan would have been easier to get, and very likely since I'd already had 20% of the needed capital. At that time, however, my only thought had been, "I'll prove myself first." Despite my success, I was always trying to do better.

It was very difficult, at first, adjusting to a start-up office. With my large staff at Ogilvy & Mather, I'd hardly had to blow my own nose! With just me and my assistant, I was having to do things I hadn't done for a long time. Fortunately, I had a solid foundation in all aspects of media.

As my business developed and grew, I found that even though I had the same work ethic, I was not obsessed. For one thing, I was no longer traveling three hours a day to and from work. Taking an hour or so for lunch (something I never did before), I found I actually got more work done. I wasn't working more, I was working smarter. I began to feel like a person instead of a machine. When I started cooking dinner, for the first time in years, my husband almost dropped dead with surprise.

My daughter is 15 now, and she's perfectly fine. My office is two minutes from her school and three minutes from home. If I have to work until 6:00 or later, she can meet me at the office and do homework. And I'm back to doing what I really love—dealing with people and taking a problem from beginning to end with them. My daughter's illness, which had seemed like a tragedy and the end of everything, was actually the beginning and absolutely the biggest blessing I have ever received.

LAUREL BURCH

Laurel Burch Design Studio, Inc.
San Francisco, California

The name Laurel Burch evokes a style of art and images intimately famil-

iar to those around the world who wear her jewelry and clothing, drink their

morning coffee from her mugs, beautify their walls with her prints, or write

love letters to friends on her note cards. This self-taught artist has created a

multi-million dollar empire of beauty and creativity expressed through

products which, as Laurel says, are meant "most of all to connect people to

one another in special ways." Her recently published book, Feline

Fantasies, features Laurel's colorful world in stories and images.

It was my grandmother's birthday and, at 8 years of age, I didn't have money to go to the store and buy her something. So I went into her backyard, gathered pine needles and wrapped them around a stick with colored threads to make a broom, and I gave that to her. My grandma lit up. She "oohed" and "aahed" and said, "Oh, this is so wonderful." What I discovered right then was that something happened between us when I was able to offer her a gift. I could gather little things of nature and put them together and give them to someone, and this special thing would happen. It wasn't that I was motivated by a passion to create something, it was that I had a passion to connect.

At age seven, my bones had started breaking, due to what was only later diagnosed as a rare bone disease. What it meant to me was that my very dwelling place was something I couldn't count on. In fact, I had little in my world that I could count on. My parents divorced when I was very young, and I had many homes and many sets of step-parents before I set out on my own at the age of fourteen. In all the ways children around me were being measured by their accomplishments—competition in sports and academic grades—I fell short. So from a very early age I went inside to find a place of comfort and support and stability. That's when I discovered my imagination as a safe place, as a sanctuary. I discovered that interwoven with all the challenges, there was only one me—and that also meant that there was only one of everybody else. It was a wondrous discovery. Over the years I learned I could share that special place inside me with others. In the hospital as a child, I made things for the other children and told them stories. Enormous joy came when I had something I could give. The more I was able to offer, the more important it became for me to find tangible ways of sharing that place inside with other people.

However, I didn't know that's what I was looking for at 17 when I was hammering metal wire into earrings on the back of an old black frying pan and selling them for $2 on the streets of Haight-Ashbury in the '60s. Like everybody else around, I was trying to figure out who I was. I had a lot of voices in my head saying, "You're not educated. You don't have a family. You have a body that doesn't work. You don't have this or that." I could hear my father's voice saying, "You're nothing but a hippie. You're never going to amount to anything. What makes you think you can succeed?" And I was alone with those voices. I had lived so much in my inner world in order to survive that I didn't know how to fit with other people. I felt connected to other cultures and other times, but I felt isolated from my own.

I would gather together different things, like Native American beads, and bones that had once been part of a living animal, and coins from other lands that I could only dream about. They seemed to have magic in them. I found that if I took all of these things and twisted them and wove them and strung them together and put them on myself—often underneath my clothes so they would be close to me—I had a sense of belonging, of being connected to those other worlds and other times.

Sometimes I would wear one of these pieces on the outside of my clothes and someone would come up to me on the street and say, "Where did you get that? It's wonderful." I was so humbled by the fact that someone would find value in it for them, and I would take it off and give it to them. I gave everything away at first. So one day when someone asked me to come to a gathering at their house to *sell* my jewelry, it seemed like a sacrilege. These were gifts, they were about self-worth and about offering.

When I was nineteen, my daughter Aarin was born, and I got a job as a salesgirl at Cost Plus for $1.25 an hour, while paying a babysitter fifty cents an hour. Sometimes I'd wear earrings I had made to work, and customers would say, "I'd like the kind you have on." Soon one of the buyers asked if I could make some to bring in and sell, and so I started making earrings on the weekend. But the inner voices were loud: "Who do you think you are to make something and ask money for it!"

I began to see that those voices were defeating me, that I was getting in my own way. I thought, "If I have voices in me, saying 'I don't . . . I won't . . . I don't know how . . . ,' I must also have others that say, 'It's okay, you do know.'" Something in me just said, "Stop! Be quiet!" to those defeating voices, and started to recognize and speak aloud what I did have. I had a lot of heart and passion and courage. If I could have just one person who believed in me, just one, then I could find a way to offer something in this world. And so I made *myself* that one person. I stepped out of that defeat and got behind myself. I remembered the courage it required to take the first step on a leg that had been broken, believing that somehow healing had taken place.

So I began in my kitchen, pounding out earrings on that old frying pan. But it never would have occurred to me that I was trying to be a businesswoman. I didn't have a clue what "business" meant; I was just trying to survive, by my own means. My first employee was someone who came knocking on the door selling vitamins. She had heard me hammering and, trying to get in the door to make a sale, she asked what I was doing. When she saw the trays of beads, she was fascinated. As we talked, she started stringing some beads to help out, and it just evolved into her working for me—for ten years. I hired other friends and we worked in a garage together. I was always just flying by the seat of my pants, and I made so many mistakes. But I remember distinctly feeling the presence of my own self behind me, moving me forward. I loved the satisfied feeling of creating something of value to others which also enabled me to take care of myself and my daughter.

The elements that have made my business possible are a weaving of destiny, magic, good fortune, sheer will and perseverance, and determination—far more than talent. While there is a part of me that has always loved to create harmony and beauty, I was not born an artist. I have no portfolio of my artistic creations as a child. I never said, "I want to be an artist when I grow up." It was rather that what I wanted to offer needed a form. In the course of sorting out who I was in the world, I found that it was necessary to find some voice and some vehicle. So I taught myself to be an artist, and my art taught me what my voice was.

As the years went by, I became aware that people felt the magic in these pieces I designed, and they would give them to someone else, recognizing the kindred spirit they shared. It became very clear to me that my purpose in life was to create tangible symbols of connectedness and of meaning. It was the work of mythology that storytellers and folk artists have carried on for thousands of years. And each creation is just a little seed that becomes something unique to each person who touches it.

I designed a piece called "Inner Spirit," with two figures, a smaller inside a larger. One evening after a talk I gave, a woman came up to me, holding this piece in her hands. She started crying as she told me that she had been abused by her father as a young girl. As an adult, she had tried to come to terms with it through years of therapy, but her father had died before it was resolved. "For me, this is a symbol of forgiveness," she said about the piece, "of my having reached the point at which—despite whatever it was that had happened to my father that could cause him to do such a thing—I have finally found my own place in the world." She had always been looking for someone who would take care of her, who would be her protecting father. But now for her, *she* was the larger figure in the symbol, and her father was the figure inside her heart that she needed to embrace. She could finally say to him, "You're in me and we're part of each other, and I forgive you." That figure meant that to her.

Meeting this woman, and others who told me about the meaning and connection they had found in my work, was why creating a business became so important to me. It wasn't an end in itself, it was the way. I had to create a structure to support the work I needed to do. Remaining aware of that has given me the courage to make the mistakes, to fall flat on my face when something I proposed didn't work, and still carry on. Even when the business began taking 90% of my time and energy—me, a high school dropout, going around with a briefcase, meeting with bankers—what gave me the courage was believing in my mission.

I know that there is a unique and precious and valuable individual spirit and voice in everyone, and it may not even be recognizable as a specific talent. But if we recognize what it is we're passionate about and go with that, the universe has a wonderful way of giving us what we need. I think that a lot of women, when they consider creating a business, think they have to have it all figured out beforehand, or else it won't happen. But without having a plan, without knowing what I was doing, I have created not just one but many multi-million dollar companies. For some people it works well to have a plan, but those who might be more intuitive and not know how to make a plan can also manifest their vision and find their way.

SISTER ROSALIND GEFRE

Professional Massage Center
School of Professional Massage
St. Paul, Minnesota

Sister Rosalind Gefre is a Sister in the Catholic Order of St. Joseph of Carondolet. She is also a professional massage therapist, teacher of therapeutic massage, and a popular public speaker. In opening her first massage center in 1983, Sister Rosalind had to overcome misunderstanding in both her religious and secular communities. In the process, she rewrote city ordinances and achieved national and international recognition. Sister Rosalind now has five centers offering therapeutic massage and two schools teaching professional massage therapy. Every day, her employees also work on-site in local corporations. Sister Rosalind and her staff are regulars at games of the St. Paul Saints—a Northern League baseball team—providing neck and shoulders massage to baseball fans.

If I hadn't gone home to take care of my dying mother, I might never have entered the field of massage therapy. It was the early 1970s, and I had been working as a nurse and living in Fargo, North Dakota, with my community, the Sisters of St. Joseph. When my aged mother needed 24-hour care, I went back to the small town where she was living, a few hours away from where I had grown up. She was in a great deal of pain and asked me one day to take her to a local massage therapist. As a family we had always more readily gone to local chiropractors than to medical doctors, so massage was something familiar to us, although I had never experienced it myself. In the therapist's office, I saw a leaflet on something called "foot reflexology." Out of curiosity, I read it, thinking this might be something I could do to help my mother. I asked the therapist, "Rose, is there anything to this?" She said, "Yes, why don't you take the class and then come and practice with me." Talk about God working!

After taking the class, when I arrived back at her office, Rose decided to give me a massage instead of us practicing. Before I knew it, I was up on the table. When she worked on me, something amazing happened. For about 25 years I had had persistent internal chest pains, often walking the night with pain. Every year I spent between one and six weeks in the hospital, with doctors trying to diagnose the cause. That massage actually put an end to the pains. I immediately knew that God was calling me to do massage, and I began to search out how I could learn it.

I couldn't leave my mother to go to school, so I searched and searched to find a way I could study at home while caring for her. I was told about a blind gentleman in town who had studied Swedish massage in Chicago many years before, and I ended up studying with him. He didn't charge me anything. He just said, "I want to do this so that you can take care of your mother."

Of course, I still considered myself a nurse, and I assumed I would continue with that work, which I loved. But it was as if God took hold of me, and I knew inside that I could never go back into nursing. I remember calling a friend who lived in Fargo and saying, "Mary Ann, I'm not sure what to do. Something has happened inside me—I don't know why, but I cannot go on being a nurse." Mary Ann said, "Don't worry—we don't know what the future holds, but we know who holds the future." That gave me courage to live by faith and believe that when the time came, God would open the doors, whatever they would be.

My mother died after three years, and I returned to my community in Fargo hoping now to do therapeutic massage. But this was the 1970s and massage was not at all popular in that area. The hospital where I had worked as a nurse refused me, saying, "You can come back as a nurse but not as a massage therapist." I had no idea what to do. I had always been assigned my jobs by the community, and I didn't know how to go out in public to find work. The other sisters were saying, "Why don't you stay with what you are— a nurse?" Nursing was nice, and in their eyes, massage was definitely not nice, but I knew it was a pure gift from God for healing. I knew I felt God's call, and I had to keep pursuing it.

When I called the family YMCA, hoping they might need a massage therapist, I was told they already had someone. As I contemplated what to do next, I began hearing a voice inside me saying very insistently, "Call the Y. Call the Y." I thought, "That's crazy. I've already tried that." The words only got louder until I felt as if they were almost screaming in my mind. Finally, just to shut them up, I called. The person who answered the phone that time responded to my question with "Yes! When can you start?"

I continued working at the Fargo family YMCA for eight years, until I got word from my religious superiors that I was to transfer to St. Paul, Minnesota. I really did not want to go. I cried a great deal, and prayed and prayed. But of course I accepted. I always believe that whatever happens, the Good Lord is in charge. When I arrived here, my superiors didn't seem to know what to do with me, but at least they had gotten me out of massage. It was so difficult for them to understand how a Sister could do that. For many people at the time, massage seemed to be associated with the red light district—prostitutes using "massage parlors" as a front.

For about a year I was assigned to work in the kitchen at a home for retired Sisters, helping with cooking and cleaning. Although I again believed that God's hand was in it, it was the last thing I wanted in all my life, and it was a very sad time for me. A few sisters there believed in massage, so on my free time at lunch or after work, I would massage them. Eventually, new people were appointed as my superiors, and I went to them to ask again if they would allow me to start doing massage as my work. Even though many in my religious community were still opposed, my superiors gave me the approval to do so.

I found a little place to rent with two rooms for massage and an office. I had passed the exam for getting my license, and so it was my understanding that I was ready to start. Later I learned that the

licensing requirements for opening a massage business also entailed fingerprints, a mug shot, and a $500 fee. They also had regulations about what to wear, when to open, and when to close. These were clearly meant for massage parlors, and I was being classified in the same group! There was simply no way I was going to submit to that, and thus began my struggle with the City of St. Paul. The city licensing department informed me that if I did not comply with their requirements, I would be closed down . . . and I was.

I had been open for two weeks when officials from the licensing department appeared. When they asked to see my permit, I showed them my massage license. They said "That's not enough. You're closed." My heart just sank. I had finally gotten the okay from my superiors, and now here I was shut down. I went home feeling so hurt that I didn't tell any of the Sisters. One evening shortly after, someone called from the largest city paper. They had heard what happened, and they wanted to ask me why I did massage. I told them that throughout the Scriptures, Jesus was always touching those he healed. "Massage basically heals people with touch, and so that's what I do," I said.

The next morning the Sisters opened the newspaper and there was the headline: "Nun's Massage Parlor Closed." That was the beginning of the real struggle. I had been living with a few other Sisters in a seminary where priests were trained. All of a sudden, for me to live there was scandalous. Even though my superior did say I could stay, there was too much pressure from others. In trying to find somewhere to move to, I called three other places where Sisters in my community lived, but none would take me. I finally found a place to house-sit for the next year.

I also had to appear in court. The presiding judge said, "I can't imagine a Sister of St. Joseph being dragged here before me! But since you're here, I'll have to deal with you." Thank God, he understood what I was doing, told me to go open my Massage Center and in thirty days appear before another judge. I went back to work, but I felt so alone. I used to cry when I was doing massage. Clients would say, "Sister, you've had that cold for so long," and I would say, "I don't know why it's not going away." It was such a deep pain not to be accepted for what I knew I had to do.

The second judge was also sympathetic, and so I was able to continue working. However, even though I now had approval, I still had to face misunderstanding in those around me. It is astounding to recall the kinds of things that happened during those early years. There were times when I would sit down at a table to eat with other Sisters, and some of them would pick up their trays and walk away.

But eventually therapeutic massage took its rightful place. I began working with the city council to rewrite the local ordinances, and I have been working to create standard regulations statewide, so that massage therapy will not be subject to restricting ordinances in various locales. We currently serve clients from all walks of life in our five branches of the Professional Massage Center. Our two Schools of Professional Massage, in St. Paul and in Rochester, Minnesota, have a growing number of students. We strive to teach the best in therapeutic massage, with a strong base in anatomy and physiology. The growing public support really taught the other Sisters the value of massage, so slowly their attitude has shifted. We now even have Sisters going to our school. Like any other Sister, I give my salary over to the community and receive back what I need to live, so what I do benefits all of us.

Faith brought me through all this. I have kept believing that Jesus really wanted me to be doing massage and that he would lead me through it all. That's what gave me the strength to move on. I know that God created our bodies to function in health, and that massage can help. Massage now no longer carries the stigma it once did, and sometimes I think that maybe God needed somebody the public could trust to bring about that acceptance — perhaps a Sister could do that better than a layperson. Whatever it is, I am just grateful that God has used me in this way.

ANN RUETHLING

Chinaberry Book Service
Spring Valley, California

Chinaberry started as a mother's passion to find good books for her children and grew into a mail order business with more than six million dollars in sales in 1996. In her catalogs Ann describes outstanding books she has discovered for toddlers to teens (along with a few for their parents). Her reviews read like letters from a close and caring friend whom you would readily trust with the minds and hearts of your children. The success of Chinaberry has allowed Ann to launch her next dream, a catalog for women, entitled Isabella: Books and Tools for the Gentle Crafting of the Spirit.

For my daughter Elizabeth's first birthday, one of my best friends sent her a book of Mother Goose nursery rhymes. That was the first book I opened in front of her. The rhymes were the same ones I'd grown up with. The lilting rhythms are so fun to read that it hardly seems to matter what they're about. But as I read them to Elizabeth, I found I was disturbed by the lack of caring and respect expressed in many of them. Peter Pumpkin Eater kept his wife in a pumpkin shell. The old lady who lived in the shoe beat her kids soundly before she put them to bed. I changed the words on some of them. The old lady "kissed them all soundly," but I never could come up with anything for Peter Pumpkin Eater. We just skipped that page.

I started going to the library to see what kind of books for children I could find there. I would bring home armfuls and go through them before reading them to Elizabeth. When we traveled to bigger towns, I would go into the library or bookstores to see what they had. We couldn't afford to buy books, so I started keeping notes on index cards about the ones I liked and at what age I wanted to introduce Elizabeth to each book. I didn't have the kind of background that would lead me to think I knew what kind of reading would be good for kids—no younger brothers or sisters, no classes on child development. I just knew what I wanted my child to hear and see in a book.

We were living at the time in a small town in Oregon. My husband Ed and I, ready for new horizons, had moved there from Colorado before Elizabeth was born. Our first winter in Oregon, however, we thought we'd made a terrible mistake. It seemed always to be raining in Port Orford. The fortunate part eventually turned out to be that Elizabeth and I spent a lot of time indoors, reading books, while Ed was out working as a carpenter. My stack of index cards kept growing. When it was about three or four inches high, I began to realize how much time and work had gone into it. By that time I knew that there were a lot of books for children that were flat-out terrible, and there were a lot of really wonderful ones. I thought, "If parents could just feed those wonderful books into the hearts and minds of their children, the world would have to become a better place."

I decided I was going to make all this information available as a service to other people by putting out a newsletter or catalog. Initially, I didn't have any intention of selling the books myself—until I realized that if people were living in a small town, as I was, they weren't going to be able to find these wonderful books I was recommending. I decided to stock a few of each, so that if people couldn't get them anywhere else, they could get them from me. In Elizabeth's bedroom, in our little house, Ed built a wall of shelves. Most of them were used for toys, but two were put aside for my inventory.

I still didn't have a name for my catalog. The only thing I could come up with was about unicorns, and I knew unicorns were already reaching critical mass. One day I told my best friend in town—who came over regularly with her little son for pancakes or waffles—that if she came back the next day with a name for this catalog I was doing, I would serve her fresh strawberries with her waffles! The next morning she told me about a story that she had loved as a child called "Under the Chinaberry Tree." She loved that name, Chinaberry. I added "Book Service"—and gave her the strawberry waffles.

The first catalog listed 116 books. My mom lent me $2000 to pay for the printing of 400 catalogs and for a little ad in *Mothering Magazine* that said "Positive and enriching books for children. Free catalog." Requests for catalogs and orders for books started trickling in. One order a day at that point was big time, and if it was for twenty dollars, I felt truly blessed. Elizabeth who was two by then helped me pack these orders on the kitchen table after breakfast. One day I opened the silverware drawer and thought, "Where could all my spoons be?" It turns out that Elizabeth had been sticking dirty spoons in with the orders. Nobody ever wrote to tell me about that, but what they did write was amazing. Most orders came in with letters saying how connected people felt to me just from reading the catalog. I was astounded. I always sent a personal note back to them when I sent out the order.

So Chinaberry was personally satisfying, but it certainly wasn't making money. I was using our grocery money at times to mail packages. Ed was basically humoring me, knowing I had a creative side that needed to be expressed. But it was dire. Work wasn't very forthcoming for him, and we were hitting rock bottom. But I *had* to do this—mainly because I really wanted to give people something to change the world, and this was my avenue.

After a couple more years in rainy Port Orford, Ed and I knew we had to find some sun, just to keep our sanity. The day we arrived at our new home in San Diego, a call came from my mother's doctor. I flew back East with the kids and stayed with her as she was dying. This meant that Ed had to move us into our new house and to fill Chinaberry orders. There were still only about two a day, but when he opened them, he began to see the kind of letters I was receiving, and he realized that there was more to this endeavor than just selling books. He saw that I was providing something intangible—a connection to a kindred soul by mail. By the time I got back he had made a decision. Instead of taking the job he had found in San Diego, he suggested that he study up on the mail order business to see how to get Chinaberry off the ground. The inheritance money from my mom, a total of $60,000, would support the process.

Ed dove in. We learned that renting mailing lists rather than display ads was the way to advertise. We filled our garage with inventory. And we continued to plod along. Then sometime around 1985, the business took off. The children of baby boomers were now the age our books were geared to, and we were in the right place at the right time for mail order.

It was still just the two of us, however, and we were strained to the max. I'm a morning person, Ed's a night person. I would get up at 4:00 a.m., just as he was going to bed, and I'd put in a couple of hours of work before the children woke up. Ed would get up around 10:00 or 11:00 in the morning and we'd set to work on Chinaberry while keeping track of the children at the same time. But we were starting to feel guilty—our children were there, but we weren't really available to them. After one overwhelming holiday season, we realized we couldn't handle all the orders ourselves. We hired our first employee, Mary, and business continued to grow. When zoning regulations put a crimp on the 18-wheelers screeching down our residential street to deliver pallets of books, we moved our inventory out of our garage and into a warehouse. Chinaberry has continued growing to the point where we now have fifty employees and annual sales of over $6 million. When I look back and see how we started, it seems a miracle. I guess it was meant to be.

As our customers continue to tell us, Chinaberry is a gift to them as well. We still get personal letters with our orders. We have an entire wall in a hallway at our offices covered with letters from people telling us how important Chinaberry is to their family. We also have a Wall of Shame, covered with jackets and titles of the incredibly horrible books that have come in for review. There are about five to eight thousand children's books published every year, and I would say truthfully for every book that's in the catalog, we've gone through about 100 to find it.

I still look for books that are positive, that speak of the oneness of everyone on the planet, that show people who are being brave and true to their highest selves—even when they're up against something really creepy. I like books that are humorous, and books that are reassuring, that tell children that they are loved no matter what, that they are respected, that their concerns are taken to heart. I don't have a checklist; basically, they just have to feel right in my gut, something I would have been pleased to read to my own kids—because just as I felt at the beginning, Chinaberry is not just a business, it's a service, and I still hope that by reading books to our children that show people caring for and respecting each other, we can make a difference in the world.

BELINDA GUADARRAMA

GC Micro
Novato, California

GC Micro has grown from a small software distributor into an award-winning supplier of computer products to defense, aerospace and commercial enterprises, with current revenues approaching $25 million annually. In the process of growing her business, Belinda Guadarrama confronted the Department of Defense, winning a lawsuit in favor of contracts for small and minority-owned businesses. Among numerous awards, she was the 1993 U.S. Hispanic Chamber of Commerce's Businesswoman of the Year and has received the Small Business Administration's Award for Excellence in 1991 and 1996.

I arrived at my job one morning to find a note on the door announcing that the owner had closed the business. Shocked, I stood out in the parking lot with the other nine employees who had worked there, all of us wondering what we should do. I had been hired a year before to reorganize the business, a software distributor, which had been losing money. After months of establishing procedures, clarifying job descriptions, and organizing accounts, the company had finally arrived at the point where it was just beginning to run smoothly and efficiently—and suddenly . . . this. I felt at a complete loss. I had moved to the area from Texas and had spent the previous year entirely focused on work. I hadn't had time to create a network of local connections. It would mean hunting for a job in San Francisco with no contacts, and I knew that would be tough.

I made a quick mental assessment of what my options and skills were. Based on the work I had done that past year, I realized I had a very clear understanding of what it would take to run a business of this kind. I had already been planning how to move the company in a new direction. Why not just continue with that plan on my own but on a smaller scale? It had never occurred to me before that I might run my own business, but the day I stood there in the parking lot, outside those closed doors, GC Micro was born. At that moment, starting my own business actually looked much easier than trying to find a job in a city where I knew scarcely anyone.

My parents used to say to me, "If you want something to happen, you're the one who has to make it happen. It's up to you." Throughout my life, once I have made a decision, I go forward with it. If it doesn't work, I know I can always adjust it, but it does no good to simply say, "I don't know what to do." As General Patton said, "A well thought out plan today is better than a perfect plan tomorrow." I guess years of practicing that attitude gave me the confidence to do what I did next.

I met with a couple of the other employees to ask if they might be interested in working with me in a new company, and I explained my idea. They liked it, and I went home to begin. The money I had from the recent sale of my condominium back in Texas, along with the retirement fund I had accumulated over the years, became my pool of working capital. Within a week, I had arranged with the owner of the previous business to sublet a small office space in the same location and with my two former co-workers, now employees, I launched GC Micro.

The strategy I had been devising for the previous company was to target large local companies and market directly to them. I proceeded with this plan, now for my own company, and sent out letters to about 200 corporations, asking them to contact me if they were interested in the software and services we offered. We got a very good 10% initial response. Over time as our customers asked us if we could supply them with other items, we added on peripherals and computer systems in response.

GC Micro grew slowly and steadily. I only took on as much business as I knew we could handle and service with a high satisfaction level. Because I had worked for so many years within the large bureaucracies of Texas state government, I understood exactly what the corporate mentality was like. When I went out and marketed directly to corporations, I knew how to dress, how to present myself, and the types of materials that spoke to them. I let them know that I understood the intricate politics and levels of decision-making involved in the corporate structure, so they would feel comfortable dealing with me.

However, as a small business owned by a woman and a minority, I continually came up against assumptions and lack of trust from the corporate world. When I went to a bank to borrow $5000 for the business, the banker broke into laughter and said, "There is absolutely nothing we can do for you." They didn't even give me an application. As we expanded into new product lines, one representative from a major computer company outright stated that, in his personal opinion, a minority- and woman-owned business would not have the management or the financial background to be able to represent their product in the way it should be represented. It took all the tact I had gained over the years to explain why I felt he was wrong. Ultimately, GC Micro did receive the authorization to carry their product. Throughout all of this, I was aware that we were not only establishing a track-record for ourselves but were also doing so for other small, women-owned and minority-owned businesses in general.

Perhaps it was that perspective that led me to put the expansion of my business on hold for a while as I pursued a major lawsuit. In 1985, when GC Micro had been just starting, I knew I needed to work with major corporations, not only so we could count on getting paid but also because most of them have an outreach program specifically geared to forming contracts with small businesses. I focused on defense contractors, the group likely to have the most money at that time, and therefore the most potential contracts. I got lists of names and began sorting out which corporations to contact. An employee of the Defense Logistics Agency suggested I request, under the Freedom of Information Act, a government document detailing the dollar amount of each government contract, the contractor involved, and the goal established for the percentage of subcontracts to be awarded to small and minority businesses. I could then target for marketing those companies falling short of their goals.

I began noticing that the goals negotiated on the contracts I reviewed were consistently below the federal statutory guidelines of 5% for minority-owned businesses. Moreover, every company was falling short, even on their 1% or 2% goals, and they weren't incurring any of the supposed legal consequences. When I tried to find out specifically why the F-22 Stealth fighter contract had a goal of less than half of 1%, I was not only dismissed with an inadequate answer, I was also prevented from further access to the documents which I had been requesting and receiving for two years. Something was very wrong, and I felt compelled to respond. GC Micro had nothing to gain from my confronting the issue, since we didn't supply the kind of high tech services needed on that particular project. We, in fact, stood to lose business by alienating defense contractors. But for me, this was a matter of right or wrong. I went to my U.S. congressional representatives and to business associations with the information I had. I put out a press release, and eventually the issue escalated into a federal lawsuit—GC Micro Corporation vs. the Defense Logistics Agency.

Sustaining the suit was emotionally very draining, and sales at my company dropped dramatically for about a year or two. It was often a solitary battle, but near the end of the process, a group of business owners and members of the Hispanic, Black, and Asian Chambers of Commerce came together so effectively that at every hearing, 95% of the people in the courtroom were supporters. Winning the case not only procured hundreds of millions of dollars worth of contracts for small and minority-owned businesses, but I think it sent a message to large corporations that small businesses are organized. I think many more individuals now realize that they too can make the kind of real changes that benefit themselves and other small and minority-owned businesses. The good reputation of GC Micro did win out, and we moved forward again, diversifying into the commercial arena as well. We have since received numerous awards and acknowledgments from some of those same corporations who were against my lawsuit originally.

I think our success has also been due to the fact that I went into this business not because I love computers but because it seemed like a very smart business decision. Many times people start a business based on something they enjoy doing without considering whether there is a viable market for their product. Certainly there are people who have, throughout their lives, demonstrated good instincts for making wild, creative ideas happen, but you have to look at your personality and your skills to see what your own capacity is. I am definitely the more methodical, logical type, and my way was to make a sound business decision. The decision I was forced to make in the parking lot that day was indeed the right one. GC Micro is very successful, and although having my own business is very life-consuming, it is also very rewarding.

BARBARA BECKMANN

Barbara Beckmann Designs, Inc.
San Francisco, California

Barbara Beckmann turns fabric into patterned works of art. Her florals, stripes, latticeworks and abstracts are handpainted and screened with non-toxic pigments on handwoven silks and linens, pure cottons and top-grade leathers. Beckmann fabrics and wall hangings grace palaces, private jets, exclusive hotels and the creations of noted fashion and interior designers around the world. Starting with her first company, Barbara Beckmann Designs, incorporated in 1983, she has expanded into One Of A Kind by Barbara Beckmann, the Santa Rosa Collection, and her latest, the Ecos Collection created with innovative environmentally-safe production methods.

In order to succeed in an industry like fashion, you have to see the big picture as well as know every tiny detail of the field. In other words, it's about knowing the context. That's what I had been learning in my eighteen years working in textile design before I started my own business.

The early years were about a lot of nitty-gritty work—knowing how to get fabric printed, whether in two yards or two thousand yards. When I was starting out, I always worked for companies where I knew I could learn something. So even though I could have earned three times more as a waitress, I never took a job as one. That wasn't what I wanted to learn in my life. I never did anything that wasn't going to lead me to my goal.

The first textile job I got was with a really good firm in New York's Seventh Avenue fashion district. Being 22 years old, I assumed of course that I knew it all. I came to the job with degrees in painting and printmaking. I had been showing my paintings in some major New York galleries. The job turned out to be literally washing paintbrushes for a very old lady who was a superb colorist. At the time I thought the job was just terrible—washing her brushes and having her tell me what to do. Looking back, however, I can see how valuable that experience was and how much I learned.

You can learn a great deal on a job while not spending your own money. You learn the ins and outs of how things are done and how they're produced. I also learned how to see quality. I was sent out into the stores to buy very expensive goods to see what I would choose and whether my taste level met the criteria for the kind of employee they needed. I learned how to spot trends and how to deal with changes in style and fashion. That, I think, is the basis of any business—to know how to make the right changes as quickly as possible.

I probably never would have started my own business if I had stayed in New York. I had a fabulous agent there who was getting me work with all the major houses, and I was very successful. Then my husband got a job in San Francisco. In the '70s there was almost nothing going on out here in my field, so I had to make the best of it. I took a job with the only design business around in order to learn about the local printers and suppliers and how to get things done in this area. I continued to freelance for New York houses, and began designing for fashionwear companies in San Francisco. All during this time, I continued making friends with interior designers. I belonged to a professional organization and attended conferences and lectures. I was finding out who the major players were. So the day I went into business on my own, I was already well-connected and very knowledgeable.

But the way I actually started the business was almost a joke. I had come up with the idea of making handpainted wall hangings. My New York agent had died quite suddenly, and these were something to fill the gap and keep my work going. I was also curious to see what might happen with these wall hangings, so I had a small show of several at a local college where I was teaching textiles. One day a woman who had seen the show approached me to say she wanted to introduce me to some people she knew. It turned out they owned some of the more beautiful fabric showrooms on the West Coast, and they wanted my wall hangings. Soon they started selling them on a daily basis, and I was having to replace them constantly. I look back on this now and see that it was very unusual, a stroke of luck to get that kind of recognition so immediately. That was the beginning.

I moved into a very big apartment, so I would have room to work. I bought ten catering tables, set them up on the terrace and started designing my own fabric. Since I'd been at this for eighteen years, I had drawers full of designs. I just took some of my ideas and developed them in the direction I wanted them to go. I was determined never to paint another cabbage rose! It seemed as if I had painted ten million of them for various companies. Although I had learned a great deal by creating the kind of look and design that each company had wanted, I had my own definite look. I knew the market I was interested in designing for, and I was determined to go after it. I think knowing who your market is and how you want to approach it is everything. You have to decide what your niche is and stick with it. Mine was the high-end commercial showroom catering to the exclusive design trade.

I ended up painting throughout the apartment and had cloths in various stages of design draped over everything. I was doing every stage of the process myself—painting, silkscreening, finding materials that matched, marketing the products to the interior designers, doing all the bookwork at night.

One day a woman came into one of the showrooms that carried my work and asked if she could order ninety yards of fabric to match one of my wall hangings. The man she spoke to—who also happened to be a friend of mine—said yes and took her money. When he called to tell me about the request, I flat-out told him, "I don't do that." I had created the wall hangings as one of a kind and just hadn't thought of repeating the design. But knowing I could manage this very quickly, he said, "You have to do it!" It was this incident that turned things around and got me going as a real business.

I had enough money from that order, along with a small amount I had saved, to move into a studio. I got a great lease in a low-rent district down by the waterfront. At first I shared with another artist, but within two months I was able to move into my own space. Meanwhile, I was working fourteen-hour days to get together my own line of handpainted fabrics. Once I started putting them in local showrooms, people from showrooms in other cities began asking for my line.

I really hadn't been sure at the time whether a business promoting my own line was going to work out or not. I had absolutely no background in marketing or sales, and that's basically what I needed to do—show my new work to interior designers when they came to the showrooms. For four or five years, I made sure I went to every single market in our industry—that's two markets a year in each major city. I knew I had to be out there if I was ever going to get any place in this field. I had to know who was doing what where, and they had to know who I was. But that schedule meant I had to do my design work, fabric sampling, and shipping on the weekends. During the week I was on the road traveling, getting ideas, spending time with people I met at the markets, going to Europe, staying on top of trends, and selling my ideas to clients.

I still travel constantly, nationally and internationally. I have showrooms in about twenty cities in the U.S., and I'm on the road about twice a month. I keep a book of every textile market that's happening, and where the people attending it stay, and I try to be in the right place at the right time. At this point, the design part of the business is minimal. Running the business and marketing it are 95% of the work. At first that was a big surprise. I didn't start my company in order to have a business. My only motivation was designing, and being good at it. But actually I think marketing can be just as creative as sitting down and designing.

It's hard to start a business, and it's hard to sustain one. There certainly have been times when I wasn't sure whether I wanted to continue. Some days I go in and say, "Oh, I wish I could sell the business tomorrow." It's very hard work. But I was determined, and I always have been. I just knew what I wanted to do, and I remained very focused. That's what it takes.

POLLY HELM

Pendleton Cowgirl Company
Eugene, Oregon

For two decades, from 1910 to about 1930, cowgirls throughout the country competed and exhibited at rodeos —riding broncos and wild steers, roping, racing and trick riding. Pendleton, Oregon, Polly Helm's home and heritage, was and still is host to one of the biggest rodeos in the nation. Discovering these "ordinary women who chose to do extraordinary things" became the inspiration for Polly Helm's life and her business. Her line of notecards, calendars and art prints, accompanied by historical sketches, highlight this largely unknown era of women's history, featuring photographic images of authentic American heroines. This original line has been expanded to include images of rodeo cowboys and Native Americans of eastern Oregon at the turn of the century.

The grainy photograph intrigued me for years . . . a young woman in a fringed rawhide skirt, silk shirt and cowboy boots, tipping the brim of her Western hat. I first laid eyes on her when I was working as a darkroom technician in the library of the University of Oregon where I was a student in photography and filmmaking. One day my boss passed by my desk and dropped off this print, which was made from a glass plate negative he had found in the archives. For some reason, he thought I'd find it interesting.

It wasn't just the old photographic style in the print that intrigued me, but also the determination, pride and defiance in the face and stance of the woman in the picture. Etched across the photograph in white were the words: "Champion of All, Lady Buckaroo, Katy Wilkes, Round-Up, Pendleton, Ore 1916."

I grew up in Pendleton, the heartland of Oregon's rodeo culture. Every year in September, the population of the town tripled overnight, and schools were closed so we could go to the Round-Up. I loved all the excitement and activity, the parades, the pageantry and civic pride. My great-grandfather, J. J. Hamley, founded the saddle shop in Pendleton that made the elaborately-tooled, silver-mounted trophy saddles presented to winners at the Round-Up since the very first one in 1910. As a little girl, I loved going into that busy, rambling saddle shop, filled with the fresh smell of rawhide. During Round-Up, it was one of the town's main gathering places for rodeo folks and tourists.

Ironically, I grew up not knowing that some of the Hamley trophy saddles had been awarded to pioneer cowgirls in the early 1900s. By my childhood, in the '50s and '60s, information about authentic early-day cowgirls and their achievements in rodeo had been mostly lost. There was no reference to lead me to believe women had ever, or could ever, participate in the competitive events at the Round-Up. As a young girl, I knew one thing for sure: champions were men. So, years later, seeing the caption "Champion of All" on the photo of Katy Wilkes bewildered me. Unable to make the connection, I simply discounted the notion that Katy had ever been a real champion. Even so, the photograph stayed with me over the next decade, as I raised my son and worked my way through my masters degree and into a full-time job at the University. Sometimes tacked to a door frame, sometimes pinned on a bulletin board, the photograph grew tattered and old as it coaxed my curiosity to grow.

One auspicious day, as I was looking through the Women's Studies section in a bookstore, I saw a title: *The Cowgirls* by Joyce Gibson Roach. I pulled it off the shelf. A line the author wrote struck me: "The emancipation of women may have begun . . . not in the cities where women marched and carried signs and protested, but rather when they mounted a good cowhorse and realized how different and fine the view . . ." Bound in the center of this book were several half-tone photographs of real rodeo cowgirls who participated during the same years as Katy. There, in that book, I found validation for the inscription on Katy's picture, "Champion of All." Here was proof that women had competed, and indeed had been recognized as champions, not only at the Pendleton Round-Up but throughout the country.

I carried that book everywhere with me. I slept with it. I bought many copies to give away as gifts. To me, the women Joyce Roach wrote about represented joy and risk. They exhibited an athletic talent that I hadn't known existed. In my youth, athletic opportunities for girls were absent, although I had longed for them. Now here were these pioneer cowgirls who must have been among the earliest female athletes in this country.

It became my hobby to search out the work of those photographers who had documented cowgirl history. I hunted through newspapers, periodicals and books to put names to the faces. I discovered that Katy Wilkes was also known as Kitty Canutt and that, in 1916, she competed for three days in front of 30,000 rodeo fans, winning the Cowgirls' Bucking Horse and Relay Race events at the Round-Up. I was delighted to learn that she was awarded two Hamley trophy saddles in addition to the cash prize.

Maybe the spirit of these women was working on me. On the verge of turning 40, I began to question where my life was headed. When I looked around at my female peers at the University, seldom did I see anyone who really seemed happy, or inspired by, or connected to what they were doing. I felt it was time, now or never, to look at other careers and to steer my life in the direction that I really wanted it to go. I made a list of all the career areas I might be interested in, investigated them one by one, and eliminated each one as a possibility. By this time I had learned that debt and sacrifice in the name of education didn't necessarily lead to a better life.

In the midst of that soul-searching, I took a look in my own backyard and thought, "Maybe I'm already doing what I want to be

doing." Maybe my hobby might somehow become a viable business. I continued working at my job, but began in earnest to hunt for pictures and trace the history of the cowgirls in them. The Pendleton Round-Up always appeared in the life stories of these women. My own ancestors had once had a connection with them. I still had an uncle in Pendleton, although my family and I had been distanced from him since I was in my teens. I reached beyond the years and differences to ask whether he knew anything about pioneer cowgirls? "Yes," he said, "I have a postcard collection you might be interested in." He sent me all of his photographic postcards of cowgirls, a collection that had been started by my great-grandparents in the heyday of rodeo. On the flipside of many of the cards were notes about the person or event in the picture. These images, which had been passed down in my family through the generations, became the bridge between me and my past, and between me and my future.

I sensed that the heroines who meant so much to me might also mean something to others. How could I share the things I had found? I figured I could make the information most accessible and affordable to others in the form of notecards, with a picture on the front and history on the back. For a couple of dollars, any woman could own a little piece of her own American heritage.

I consulted with a local greeting card sales rep and told her my idea for the first nine notecards, which would be Volume 1 of the Pioneer Cowgirl Series. "Oh, no," she discouraged me. "You have to have at least sixteen different images before any store will even look at what you've got." I couldn't afford a press run that big, and I doubted her advice. I went to a printer who told me it would cost $2600 to print those first nine. I had $2000 from the sale of a car. "I tell you what," he said. "If this idea flies, you can pay me the balance. If it dies, you owe me nothing." What did I have to lose? That money was all I had . . . but what was $2000 in the course of a lifetime? With the help of a friend who had the necessary design expertise, I decided to make the leap.

The first notecard in the series was, of course, the one of Katy Wilkes, a.k.a. Kitty Canutt. In the other eight cards I was able to document Mabel Strickland, Tad Lucas, Fox Hastings, Josephine Robes Sherry, Prairie Rose Henderson, Ruth Roach, and Bertha Blancett. All of these women had ridden and won at Pendleton. Every time one of those cards came off the press, it was like the birth of a child. I was just so pleased. I wanted to look at them and touch them and count them. In addition to the smell of rawhide, I have come to love the smell of fresh-printed notecards! Two perfect events to launch their existence were coming up—the 1992 Pacific Northwest Booksellers Conference in Eugene and the Pendleton Round-Up, both in the same week of September. That year it so happened that my uncle, my grandfather and great-grandfather were being inducted into the Pendleton Round-Up Hall of Fame. I called the manager of the Hamley store in Pendleton to ask if I might set up a card display there during the Round-Up. She said yes, so I had a wooden display rack made, and I headed for Pendleton.

The Hamley store is frozen in time, as is Pendleton. It's like a museum, the walls covered with old photographs of early employees, of the local Umatilla Indians, of cowboys, and of the Hamley family migration from Wisconsin to Pendleton. It's a place where history is honored. I set up the card rack and sat down in a corner to watch as people from all walks of life paused to examine the notecards. Most spent a bit of time looking and reading, and some spent a bit of money to buy one. My observations validated what I felt inside—that other people would appreciate my documentation of these authentic pioneer cowgirls.

After the Hall of Fame dinner and induction ceremony, I returned to Eugene for the Booksellers Conference, where I covered my display table with my grandmother's Indian blanket and set up my notecard rack. The response was equally encouraging.

When the inevitable choice arose between my university job and the Pendleton Cowgirl Company, the decision was clear. I was aware of women like Vera McGinnis, a stenographer in the early 1900s. When she had to choose between sitting at a desk, bound up in a corset, or joining the rodeo, she followed her heart and saddled up. Not that it had been easy for her or any of her peers, but the fact that she made the choice to follow her heart gave me a measure of permission to do work that comes from my own inner passion and makes a worthy contribution to the world.

I decided to follow an inspiring trail that eventually led me to recover a piece of my own missing heritage. In the process, I've been able to give back a piece that was missing for many others as well.

ASSUNTA NG

Seattle Chinese Post
Northwest Asian Weekly
Seattle, Washington

With a small and efficient staff of twelve, Assunta Ng publishes the only

newspaper in the nation with both Chinese and English editions. Her two

weekly newspapers feature both local and national news and have a total

distribution of 15,000. Committed to "using every opportunity as a busi-

nesswoman to develop New Girls' Networks in every segment of society,"

Ms. Ng also sponsors events for the community at large, such as her city-

wide luncheon entitled "Women of Color Empowered."

P eople say I had a lot of courage to start a newspaper on my own, but I saw that it was something that simply needed to be done. Seattle had not had a Chinese newspaper for fifty years. When Watergate happened in the early 1970s, I remember walking past long lines of people in Chinatown who were waiting to get a copy of the Chinese-language newspaper from San Francisco so they could find out what was going on. I felt so lucky that I knew the English language and didn't have to go through that. It was at that moment I decided to start a newspaper. I had never done anything like that before, but for some reason I felt confident that I could do it. Maybe if I had thought too much about it, I might have said, "Forget it. Too hard." But I just set my goals and went ahead.

Whenever I speak at women's business groups, I always tell people, "If Assunta Ng could start a successful business, so can you." Because when I look back, the way I was as a little girl was so different from what I am now. I was very shy and afraid to do anything different or unusual. I was born in China and raised in Hong Kong, in a traditional Chinese family. I was expected to find a good husband when I grew up, and that was all. As the eldest child, however, I always felt a conflict between the necessity of being independent while also being held back by my culture. The only women around me as role models were housewives, a few secretaries, nurses and teachers. I loved my mother, but I knew one thing for sure—I didn't want to end up like her. I desperately wanted to change my life.

In high school in Hong Kong, I was so timid and unhappy that I excelled in nothing. So it was a big surprise to everybody when I scored among the top 100 in the national exams for graduation. All of a sudden my family began to look at me differently, thinking I might be college material. I worked up the courage to tell them what I had been thinking about—I wanted to go to America. My family was very poor, so I made a deal with my parents that if they could give me tuition for my first year, I would take care of myself after that. At 18 I left for Portland, Oregon. I thought I would be scared to death, but when I arrived in the airport and then at the school, everything seemed beautiful to me. I had no fear, just joy. Home was far away, and there was no turning back. In a new world I started to create a whole new me.

By the time I saw that line of people waiting for a newspaper, I was married and had been teaching junior high school in Seattle for five years. I was still unsure about what I wanted to do with my life. I had always wanted to help people, but starting a business was not something I had thought about at all. I hadn't said to myself, "I want a business." Rather I said, "This community needs a newspaper." Immigrant Chinese had to rely on rumors and gossip to find out what was going on, and I thought that was no way for a community to survive and grow.

My friends and family all tried to discourage me. They said it would be a thankless job with a lot of hard work and sacrifice. They

were right in a way, but the more people said no, the more I was convinced I should do it. The more they felt this was a stupid idea, the more I wanted to show them it wasn't. One man pulled me aside and said, "You're going around saying you are going to start a newspaper. What if you have no newspaper to show in the end?" I said, "You mean what if I fail. I have nothing to be ashamed of if I fail." He looked at me as if this was a very strange response. Maybe I didn't know what failure meant, and maybe it was a good thing I didn't know. I think I worried more about what would happen if I didn't try, rather than if I would fail. Someone needed to do this paper, and if I met Obstacle A, I would deal with it and go on to meet Obstacle B.

I did meet a lot of obstacles. When I tried to rent a place in Seattle's Chinatown, the response was, "Who do you think you are, coming in and saying you are going to start a Chinese-language newspaper?" I was involved with the Asian community but I was not a part of Chinatown. Several men had already tried and failed, and now here was a woman going around saying she was doing it. I walked up and down the streets, knocking on doors, asking if there was space for rent. I didn't understand why everyone said no. It was a good thing I didn't. It turned out that almost all of the property was owned by a few men in the community. It was an old boys' network. They didn't sell to strangers, and they didn't rent to strangers. It was discouraging, but I knew I'd come up with some way to find a place.

One day on a street in Chinatown, I met a Caucasian man coming out of one of the buildings. He said, "I've seen you around quite a few times these past days. Is there something you want?" When I told him what I was doing, he offered to show me the place he had. It turned out that the city had put money into the remodeling of this particular building, so it was one of the few in the area that did not belong to that small group of property holders. When he told me the rent was $500 a month for the 500-square-foot room, I offered him $400 plus free advertising space in the newspaper. I got the place.

Even though my husband didn't approve of me starting a newspaper, he didn't stop me from using our money to pay the rent in order to get it off the ground. I had tried to get a bank loan, but I had no credentials. The banker gave me stacks of paper to fill out, but I knew that even if I filled them all in, the answer would still be no, so I didn't even bother. When you first start, no one believes in you—you have to believe in yourself. Even one success a day is enough to keep you going.

I hired an editor and began recruiting reporters to write articles. We established the publication date for our first issue and made arrangements with printers and distributors. Then the Chinese typesetting machines we were buying got lost on their way from Taiwan. The editor said that we'd better stuff the newspaper with ads since we wouldn't have time to type enough articles. I set out to sell ads, not realizing it would be so tough in a community that had not had a Chinese newspaper for so many years. They didn't even know what the function of an advertisement was anymore. They assumed that a flyer on a community bulletin board was enough to spread the word. I had to educate them.

I thought that by starting with the oldest, most successful Chinese restaurant, I would have the best chance at selling an ad, because the owner would be certain to have enough money to afford advertising. I went and introduced myself to Mr. Chin, the owner. He had heard about someone starting a Chinese newspaper. But when I asked him to advertise, his answer was, "I have not advertised for thirty years and I'm doing great. Why should I advertise now? And why for *you*?" We talked for a while, and each time I asked him why he didn't want to advertise, he answered because he hadn't done it before. It was as if starting to advertise would look like his business wasn't as successful anymore, and he would lose face. With an attitude like that, I was getting nowhere.

I finally said, "Okay, forget about advertising. You'd like to see a Chinese newspaper in the community, right?" "Right." "So you'd like to put a congratulatory message to the paper from your restaurant." It was just an inspiration. "So this is not an ad?" he asked. "Oh, absolutely not." "How much is half a page?" "$175.00." He took out the cash and put it on the table. My first ad. So then I went to other businesses and said, "Mr. Chin is advertising, so would you like to also? And by the way, he paid cash." Over four or five weeks, I collected $4000 in advertising for my first issue. The machines arrived, and we did get the issue out on time. People were very glad that there finally was a Chinese newspaper in town, although everybody complained that there was nothing to read — too many ads. Of course no one understood why.

The hardest part was keeping it up week after week after week. We had a small staff, and I had to go out and get stories myself. It was so physically demanding that I started getting sick a lot. I was fatigued, and my body had no immunity at all. But every issue got better. By the end of the first year many people began telling us, "We are American-born Chinese, and we can't read this paper." So we started a second edition in English.

The image of those people years ago standing in line just to get a Chinese newspaper is still strong in my mind. I think it helped me to get through the obstacles. Whenever I felt discouraged, that image would come up, and I would say to myself, "You remember those people waiting in line just to get a copy of the newspaper? You can't stop now. You can't turn your back on them." Whenever I met rejection, I looked at it as the group of people experiencing rejection rather than me. All along I saw it as "us" as opposed to "me." I think maybe I remembered those people so much that I forgot myself.

THERESA MARTINEZ HOFFACKER

Constant Care Dayschool
Santa Fe, New Mexico

The demand for places in Theresa's preschool was so great during her first

year in business that her family daycare for children aged 2 to 5 soon

expanded into a childcare center in Santa Fe in 1990. In 1995 she opened a

second center in Eldorado, a neighboring suburb. Enrollment averages

25–30 in each location, small enough for staff to remain close to families

and children, one of her bottom lines. The majority of the schools' income

goes into teachers' salaries. "If I pay them what they are worth," she says,

"they can do their best work, and it enables them to continue here with the

children."

In my view, children are just about the most important thing in the world. I value them greatly, and believe they deserve to be listened to and respected. There have been times when my husband and I didn't have a lot of material things, but we did have a lot of time to hold our own children and nurture them and talk to them. We are a very close family. So when I happened to see children being abused and mistreated, I just couldn't keep from responding. That is what led me eventually to open my schools.

My husband and I were living in northern New Mexico, where he had gotten a job with the state park service. Financially, the previous few years had been pretty meager, since he had lost his job as a goldsmith in Santa Fe. Our children were very little, and I was enrolled in the art program at the local college. To bring in a little extra money, I worked a few hours a week as a clerk in the local grocery store and gas station that was a kind of town center.

One day a young couple came in to get a fishing license. The girl was holding a very little baby who kept making strange moaning sounds. I said, "I think there's something wrong with your baby," and she just brushed it off with "Oh, he's been like this for a week." I felt very concerned and told her I thought she should take him to the doctor. She ignored me, and they went on shopping and applying for their license. I asked if I could hold the baby until they were finished. I held that tiny baby very close to my heart and kept on talking to him softly. By the time they left, he had stopped crying. They were going out fishing that day. The temperature outside was 104°.

The next day at work, the owner said to me, "You know that little baby you were holding yesterday? He died last night." That hit me so hard. He was only six weeks old. I had known there was something wrong with him, and there wasn't anything I could do. I felt so bad. I thought, "This is not okay. Children deserve more than this." I had been noticing other kinds of abuse and neglect as well. Children were being left crying, locked in cars while their parents were shopping. People were hitting their kids in the store and yelling at them to shut up. All of these things made me feel that I wanted to do something for children. I wanted to somehow advocate for them and make a difference in their lives.

My husband had recently been offered a job back in Santa Fe and we had decided to go. We missed home, and my oldest child, from my previous marriage, was still there, living with his father. I was one semester away from getting my Associate Degree in Art and planned to complete it in Santa Fe. But after that baby died, I said to myself, "If I can make a difference in the lives of children, I will. That's what I want to do." I decided to enroll in the Early Childhood Development program to become a kindergarten teacher. That would be a way to do something at least.

We moved into a trailer near Santa Fe and I got a job at a daycare center. After three months, I quit the job. The way it was run and how they treated the children was so terrible that I just couldn't be a part of it. I took a job as a receptionist instead. Meanwhile I applied for grants and took classes at the community college. My husband and I were both commuting into Santa Fe to work. I was working full-time during the day, attending school full-time at night, and being a mother. I was able to do so much only because my husband is very supportive and encouraging and willing to care for the children. When I was exhausted, he was there to help them with homework and get them ready for school.

My "break" from this schedule was reading the newspaper! I started noticing an ad in the classifieds under business opportunities: Preschool for Sale. Two weeks later it was still there. I had no money, but I was intrigued. So I decided to call. The woman turned out to be a realtor who had taken over the school from a friend of hers who had gone through a divorce and left town. She didn't know a thing about running a school, she was losing money, and she really wanted to get rid of it. She knew I was interested, and she was determined to do whatever she could to help me get it.

Part of what made it so appealing was that the school was located in a huge 3200-square-foot house. One side was a residence and the other side was the school. The idea of getting out of our little trailer and also no longer having to commute to work and school was attractive. "Well, what do you have?" she asked me. "Do you have anything to trade?" We had bought an acre of land from my father in the nearby town where we were living. When I told her about that, she said, "Okay, let's trade. I'll give you the school, and I'll take the land." She made money by selling the land, and we proceeded to get the school off the ground.

I was joined by two of the teachers I knew from the school where I worked when I'd first come back to Santa Fe, and several children from that place soon followed. Their parents knew me and were delighted I was starting my own daycare center. The school had only six children in it when I got it, and we immediately went

to ten. I wasn't done with my degree, so I continued going to school at night, and I incorporated everything I was learning into our daycare program. Once again, my husband and I had to tighten our belts for a while, as I received only whatever was left after paying the staff and other expenses, and sometimes that wasn't much.

By the time we'd been in business for nine months, people were calling and begging me to take their children. Because it was in a residential neighborhood, the school was licensed for only twelve. If we wanted to take more children, we would have to find another location. Once again, I was fortunate to find the right situation — someone desperate to rent a large space that was a former school. The landlord was willing to let us in without a deposit and to bring it up to code by adding the construction costs onto our monthly rent. Now we were a full-fledged childcare center.

My next center later opened with another coincidence. When my father-in-law died and left us some money, we decided to buy a house in the suburbs of Santa Fe, where the cost of living was not so high. The realtor we worked with suggested we start a school in a nearby mall that was opening.

I have been so happy to create these centers, because I know that there are a lot of children in places that are very inappropriate. Many people cannot afford quality daycare, and end up taking their children to someone in a trailer with 20 other kids sitting in front of a TV all day. One of my intentions has been to make my daycare affordable and available to those who want it. Because I grew up in this town and know what the economic situation is, when I ask the parents where they work and what they do, I can pretty much tell what they can afford, and I base their tuition on that. As a result, my centers are multicultural. We have children who are Anglo, Black, and Hispanic. We have wealthy children and poor children. In this way, they are learning that we are all equal, and that we live in a multicultural world.

My own younger children, Kelly and Benjamin, have grown up with me doing this business. We've been very fortunate that we didn't have to put them into daycare—they lived in it! When their elementary school lets out each day, they come to the Center. When they walk in the door, the little children run to them. Kelly and Benjamin are very nurturing and helpful, and they love children too. They read to them and play with them. In fact, a couple of years ago, my husband finally put his foot down and said, "Okay, Theresa, no more children on the weekend." The children at the center often wanted to come home with us and, of course, I'd say, "Sure, you can spend the night."

We are very close with the families in our Center, and we have lots of communication with the parents. The children are with us most of the day, five days a week, so it's really important that we work closely together. I am very willing to listen to my families, and we listen to the children too, of course. We hold them and hug them and kiss them. We get down on the floor and look them in the eye when we're talking. Consequently, they know that they are very important to us. Because the business has flourished, I haven't yet been able to finish the course work for my degree. But I am doing what I was preparing to do. I think this all has happened so miraculously because I really am committed to doing what is best for children.

MARCY CARSEY

The Carsey-Werner Company
Los Angeles, California

Marcy Carsey's love of television has led her to become one of the most suc-

cessful producers in history. She started her own production business in

1980, and is one of the few remaining independent television producers. In

1981, she was joined by Tom Werner, and the team has created hits such as

"The Cosby Show," which was the top-grossing sitcom of all time,

"Roseanne," "Grace Under Fire," "Cybill," and "3rd Rock from the Sun."

In addition to receiving the top industry awards, including the Emmy,

People's Choice, Golden Globe, and the NAACP Image Award, the company

has also been honored for its efforts in producing responsible television.

That first year I started my own company I kept having a nightmare in which two tall wooden doors would slam shut just as I got to them, and I would be left standing outside, pounding on them to open. That's exactly how I felt. As I struggled to make it on my own, I was terrified that I would be locked out of the corporate world I had left and end up having nowhere to go. Many times I was ready to go back and just get a job—something I could count on for income and for a more sure and tangible connection to the world of television production. My biggest challenge that first year was sticking with my intention to start my own company. I knew I couldn't go back to where I had been, and I didn't see anything else out there that would suit me. I just had to hang on.

I had been Senior Vice President of Prime Time Series at ABC, where I had worked for seven years. If the management hadn't changed, I probably would have continued there indefinitely—I hadn't been thinking about starting my own company. But when it was time to leave, I had to figure out how I would continue in television production. I knew that's where I wanted to be.

I have always loved television, and I adored it growing up. My favorite programs early on were "I Remember Mama" and "Father

Knows Best," and later, when puberty kicked in, "Maverick" and every other Western with a handsome hero. We lived in Massachusetts and my father worked in a shipyard. Nobody in my family would ever have thought about show business, let alone Hollywood and being part of *making* television.

My brother and I were the first generation in my family to go to college. I majored in English literature and could see that I had some talent at writing and acting. By the time I graduated from the University of New Hampshire at 21, I was ready for the adventure of a big city, and a couple of friends and I set off to live in New York.

When I got there, I realized to my delight that there was an actual television industry, and that you could earn a *living* doing something that was such fun. I got a job as a tour guide at NBC. The locker rooms were a hotbed of ambition—guides and pages would do anything to find opportunities for advancement. I was lucky. In a couple of months, I moved up into the position of production assistant on the "Tonight Show." That basically meant I got to do general office tasks, answer fan mail, and schlepp things around. Eventually I worked for one of the producers, but clearly there was nowhere else to go in that setting—they weren't going to promote a secretary or a gopher to being a talent coordinator.

In order to get somewhere in the industry, I first had to take a left turn—into the television department at an advertising agency. I had no intention of staying in advertising, but I was able to get a fabulous job. It was still entry level and poor pay, but the work was great. There were three of us who functioned essentially as network spies. We would find out what pilot programs were coming up on each of the networks, read the scripts and make recommendations as to which of them our clients should buy into for advertising spots. It turned out that I was right more often than wrong. You tend to be good at what you love, and I loved television.

Eight months into that job, the man I was dating got hired as a writer for "Laugh In," so we got married and moved to Hollywood together. It wasn't exactly like starting over in my career, since I'd gotten only a couple rungs up the ladder anyway, but I did have to be persistent. Through my husband, I knew that Roger Gimbel was starting a production company. He had a room full of scripts and would need someone to analyze them. I was determined to be that person. I called Gimbel, and then called and called again. I offered to read things for free, and I basically badgered him until he hired me.

I had been working there for a couple of years when I heard that ABC was looking for talented and creative people to join in a huge team effort to turn the network around. I really wanted to get a job there, but I was pregnant with my first child. I knew I would have to tell them. In my interview with Michael Eisner, who was then head of West Coast programming, I confessed that I was three months pregnant and offered to put off the hiring process until after the baby was born if he was more comfortable with that. Eisner said, "Well, my wife and I are having a baby too, and I'm coming back to work, aren't you?" That was a pretty unusual attitude in 1974. He said, "That's not a factor," and hired me.

I was delighted, because I saw the networks as the hub of the industry. It was also a scary place to be for me. I knew I would work very hard, but I have very little tact and no ability to surf the corporate waters. They would either promote me fast or fire me fast. As it turned out, I didn't get fired. During the seven years I worked at ABC, I moved steadily up through the ranks, so that by the time I left, I was Senior Vice President of Prime Time Series and responsible for developing and supervising *all* prime time series on the network. Eisner had inspired all of us to create something wonderfully juicy, vital, and diverse. But after several years, when the management changed, the magic was gone for me. I felt I could no longer continue to work at ABC. I probably would have taken another network job if there had been a terrific high level position available, but there wasn't. The only choice that appealed to me was to go out and start my own production company.

ABC didn't want to let me go. When my contract was up, they enticed me to stay for one more year by promising me, at the end of that year, a "blind series" commitment. That meant I could come up with suggestions for pilot programs which they could accept or reject. At least it would guarantee me some level of income for a short time and a context in which to work. I stayed that extra year, then set out to form my own company.

It was hard to make such a big career change. My husband and I had two kids by then, and suddenly I was no longer drawing an executive salary. Equally hard, I no longer had the support system I'd been used to. Even if I hadn't seen eye-to-eye with those I was working *for*, I did love the people I'd been working *with* everyday. And it was frightening to leave that whole system of phones and copying machines and assistants to launch and build a business essentially from nothing.

Something else scared me as well. It didn't necessarily follow that just because I was good at network programming that I would also be good at producing. Some of the skills required are similar, but I'd be selling shows instead of buying them, and subject to the questionable judgment of those buyers.

I made a deal with one of the production studios to supply me with an office in exchange for the promise that if I sold a show that required studio financing, they would be the studio to produce it. I set to work, now as a supplier of programming rather than as a network executive. My first year, 1980, was not terrific. The new ABC management and I were no more cohesive in our visions when I worked outside than when I worked inside. It also happened to be the year of a writers' strike and an actors' strike, so it wasn't a productive year for anyone. I developed a couple of projects, but none of them sold. At one point, when our money had just about run out, my husband asked, "Are we poor, or just in the throes of a cash flow problem?" We did keep our sense of humor, but it starts to wear thin when you don't have the money to get your dry cleaning out!

At the end of the first year, Tom Werner joined me. He had taken over my job at ABC, and now he was ready to leave. We had worked together as network executives for six years, and we shared a vision. We both liked to do comedy shows with a point of view, and we were more interested in quality than quantity. The value to us in being independent was that we didn't have to put on a show unless we wholeheartedly believed in it. It took us three years before we got our first successful series, which happened to be monumentally successful—"The Cosby Show." It had an eight-year run, and by the 1988–89 season, we pulled off something that no company, major or independent, had ever done—we had the top three rankings on television, for "Cosby," "Roseanne," and "A Different World."

That little girl, years before watching TV in Massachusetts would never have dreamed she would grow up to create programs for it. Based on my love of television, which started back then, I know that the key to good programming is respect for the audience. Tom and I are firmly committed to being independent producers, so that we can develop innovative, intelligent programs, not in response to what networks think might sell, but to what we know the audience deserves.

PATRICE HARRISON-INGLIS

Sweetwoods Dairy
Peña Blanca, New Mexico

Once an executive secretary in Silicon Valley with a few goats in the back-

yard for milk, Patrice Harrison-Inglis now runs a dairy farm that produces

and distributes gourmet goat cheeses in 4-oz. rounds, wrapped in biodegrad-

able packaging and bound with red paper ribbon. Sweetwoods Dairy has

now become a family enterprise in which Patrice, her husband Harrison and

sons Ben, 15, and Les, 12, daily produce and distribute various cheeses to

outdoor markets, gourmet and healthfood stores, mainstream grocery stores,

and restaurants in the Santa Fe and Albuquerque areas.

We were on the road to becoming a typical two-income family. Harrison, my husband, was working as an industrial welding inspector, and I was a secretary. And then our first child, a beautiful, healthy boy who had been delivered by natural childbirth, was diagnosed at eighteen months with an acute and aggressive form of leukemia. When we were told that Ben would have to stay about fourteen months in the hospital for treatment, Harrison and I looked at each other and said, "Well, which one of us is going to quit our job?" Until that point we had staggered our schedules so that one of us had been with Ben most of the time. There was no way we were going to leave him in a hospital now by himself, even for five minutes.

It made sense to us for Harrison to continue at his job, but having one income meant a significant shift in our lifestyle. We ended up losing our house because we couldn't maintain the payments. When Ben's treatment was over and we began wondering where to go next, someone pointed out an ad in the paper for an old cabin in the Santa Cruz mountains in California, a couple of hours from Stanford Medical Center where we had spent most of the past year with Ben. The rent was $50 a month, and the owners would waive that in exchange for us making repairs. After the intensity of the hospital experience, it sounded peaceful; it would provide us with a chance to recover together. Someone we had met in the hospital suggested that since we were living in such an isolated place and were on a reduced income, we should get a cow to provide milk for our family, and he offered us one. When I told him I was afraid of cows because they're so big, he invited me to visit his neighbors who had dairy goats. After spending a day with them, we went home with a pregnant milk goat and a library book on how to take care of her. I have not been without a milking goat ever since, and it's been more than twelve years.

The cabin was very run down, and it took a lot of work to make it livable. After a few months there, I got a job as a secretary at a large computer firm in Silicon Valley, and Harrison stayed home with Ben to continue with repairs and maintenance. During the day I worked in a high tech environment full of computers and high-powered meetings, and at night I returned to a rustic cabin without electricity or running water and took care of chickens and goats. In the mornings I took a dip in an ice cold stream before putting on my panty hose and heading out for the hour-long commute to work. I found the contrast fun and adventurous—for a while at least. By the time I began to question where I was headed as an executive secretary in Silicon Valley, we'd had a second child, another bout with Ben's cancer, and had moved down the road to a place with electricity where Harrison managed a 60-acre fruit orchard.

One day I found myself telling a friend that I had never set out to be a secretary. It was an easy job to get and a way to make a living, but I had never sought it as my life's work. Afterwards, that conversation continued to echo in my mind. I had finally said it out loud to someone. "What I am doing with my days is not my true vocation."

Around the same time, I began noticing a very elderly, white-haired woman who worked during the lunch hour at a fast food place near my job. One day I saw her leaving work in a beat-up old car, and then another day I saw her shopping in a discount market. I thought, "That is what happens to women when they get old if they don't have a great retirement plan and a profitable enterprise. That could be me." The conversation about my work and the image of that woman were catalysts that set me up for a major change.

During the six years I worked as a secretary, I'd been spending hours at home learning how to make goat cheese. My first goat had given birth to triplets, and my little herd was giving three to four gallons of milk a day. We had been drinking it, making yogurt, giving it away to neighbors, and feeding it to the dog and cat. Considering the price of goat milk in the stores, I felt it was a pity just trying to use it up. I went to the library and got a book on how to make cheese at home. I ended up feeding a lot of my experiments to the chickens, but eventually I developed several cheeses—with various herbs and garlic—that everyone really liked. My co-workers began sending me electronic mail messages ordering cheese, and so every Friday I brought in little bundles for them. I was an executive secretary who made cheese on the side.

One day Harrison said to me, "These damn goats are just a lot of trouble, and they're eating up money in feed." I told him I thought they were paying for themselves because I had been selling the cheese at work. "Prove it," he said. I started keeping a ledger sheet, balancing cost of feed, bales of hay, and rolls of fence wire with sales of cheese. I watched it for a month, then two, then the entire summer—and it turned out the goats were actually earning money. I was amazed. Maybe those questions about my life's work had an answer.

At my job I had been using a computer program to type up business plans for new products. Why not use it myself during lunch hour and make a plan for a goat cheese business? I figured out what would happen if we had twenty goats instead of five, how much cheese I could make and sell, and where I could distribute it. I figured out what kind of location we would need, what type of buildings and equipment, and what our monthly expenses would be. Harrison was intrigued and encouraged me. He was willing to help me start out by being the general contractor. I made up a condensed version of the plan and began passing it out to potential investors. I was looking for $55,000 and was so sure my dairy farm could be up and running in six months that I promised investors double their money back in quarterly payments to begin after half a year. It was a ridiculously short timeframe, but it became a driving force. My father offered half the amount as an investment contingent on my coming up with the other half from others. Four months later, by January of 1992, the money was in the bank.

Since the price of land in California was so high, Harrison went to New Mexico, where he had grown up, to scout out land with Ben. They found five acres adjacent to the Rio Grande and began building. Our younger child, Les, stayed with me while I completed my last months at work, did research on markets and distribution, and designed labels for the cheese. In June we loaded up everything we had in one end of a huge moving van and herded the goats into the other. We had to milk them several times en route. Three days later, we unloaded the van and set to work.

What the idea looked like on paper was different from what it turned out to be. I had some false assumptions based on doing my research in California. First of all, cheese making is very touchy, and in the different climate and altitude, it took six months to get the cheese even to work. The population of Santa Fe was much smaller, and I could count on selling only about a quarter as much cheese each week as I had projected. I also had to figure out which markets worked best in this new environment. The first year was a time of absolute terror for me. I lost forty pounds and felt scared to death all the time. I had burned all my bridges and had no job waiting in the wings. I cared about the people who had lent me the money and didn't want to let them down. I wanted to be successful for their sake as well as my own. Four years after I started, I have met my goal of a herd of fifty goats, have repaid the original investment, and this year will repay the doubling of the loan as I had promised.

Sweetwoods Dairy has turned into a family operation. Instead of moving on to another job as he had planned, Harrison got increasingly involved. We began homeschooling our sons who now work as part of the business. I intend to continue at the size we are, to maintain farm-based production and be able to sell everything fresh locally, rather than expanding into a bigger market.

Now that Ben is 15 and healthy, I see what a great blessing it was that we didn't climb the career ladder. That unexpected turn in the road led me to Sweetwoods Dairy and to all I continue to learn about life, love, loss, and priorities from working with dairy goats. Each and every day begins with caring for them. Their dependence on us assures that even on the most difficult days I am up early, moving in the fresh air and attending to them. At the same time, it is their milk production that brings every dime of our revenue, so we depend upon them completely. Working with the animals is truly my inspiration, and it takes 100% of my commitment. I think if it hadn't been for Ben's hospitalization and that cabin in the woods, I don't know where we would be. The two-income family now looks like such a tense and rough way to go. We have never considered it again!

CAROLYNA MARKS

Blue Rider School of Art
The World Wall for Peace
Berkeley, California

Artist and sculptor Carolyna Marks teaches art to children and adults in

her school and works with communities around the world, through her non-

profit corporation, building peace walls out of individually painted ceramic

tiles. She has created walls in Russia, Japan, Israel, and in the United

States. Because of and despite the effects of a genetic condition that impairs

her vision, Carolyna is passionately dedicated to teaching that everyone is

an artist and a peacemaker. Her forthcoming book is entitled Emotional

Wisdom: A Peace Empowerment Process for the Artist in Everyone.

One day out of the blue, I got a phone call from the head of my department at the university where I was teaching. "I have to give you a leave of absence," he said and went on to explain that I was too strong for him to feel comfortable around. I had no idea that I was a threatening woman, since my experiences with men had always been essentially positive. To me this dismissal was a real tragedy. I was so suddenly cut off from my community. I had loved teaching. Even though the pay was low, the creativity and the stimulation of interacting with my students had been wonderful and fulfilling. I cried for months.

My first step out of that painful job divorce was the Blue Rider School of Art. I decided to start my own business and to create my own community so that it couldn't be taken away from me again. I would build a studio for the school on top of my garage and convert the space below into an apartment to rent out for extra income. The school would be the focal point for a community of artists. I had already been teaching after-school art classes for children in order to provide a community for my young son, whom I was raising alone after the death of my husband. Now I wanted to expand that into classes for adults. I moved ahead, but the school's importance in my life was soon eclipsed.

I began noticing a sign in my neighborhood. Someone had painted on a fence in very large white letters: "Do something today for peace." This was 1983, the height of the Cold War. Every time I drove past that fence, I asked myself, "Now what can *I* do? How can I contribute to peace in the world?" When I looked at what brought peace into my own life, I saw that the healing energy always comes to me through my art. The heart of every creative act is to bring together opposites—wet paint to dry paper, color to barren and empty places, feeling and thought into a void. So the artist is also a diplomat who reaches out to whatever is the "other" and creates unity. I wondered, "If the artist could have a role in society as a peacemaker—not the artist in an ivory tower but the artist in everyone—what would it be? How could I make that happen?"

The previous year when I redecorated my house, I'd had a tile painting party and invited all my friends to paint tiles for my kitchen. People of all ages came and adored doing it. They couldn't wait to see their tile up on the wall. I began to think, "Why not make a ceramic tile wall—a peace wall. Instead of a wall that separates, like the Berlin Wall, this would be a wall made of love and communication." This concept of a wall was a perfect expression of that transformation of opposites and differences that is the essence of the creative act.

I set out as my goal to get 1000 tiles painted, which seemed an astronomical number. I had no idea where the wall would be, but I would begin anyway. I set up a table with tiles and paint at the Berkeley Affaire, an outdoor event to celebrate the city, and got a hundred tiles painted every day for three days. Just having to reach out and ask people, "Would you like to paint a tile for peace?" got me out of the studio and into the world. It got me out of the grief over the loss of my job and into interacting with people. This was my action to end the Cold War. Ceramic tiles last for centuries, and I figured even if we were to die in a nuclear disaster—which at that time was an acknowledged threat—at least the wall might survive as a testimony to our love of life.

I started going to various city commissions to lobby for a peace wall in Berkeley. A small team of people developed who joined me, reading poetry and doing little performances before the Parks and Recreation Commission, the Landmarks Commission and other officials. It was a very touching and romantic approach, and boundaries began dissolving. After five years of getting tiles painted at various events and many sessions of creative lobbying, I had *three* thousand tiles, and the commissions had agreed to provide money to tear down an old wall in a downtown Berkeley park, and to build a new one—a Peace Wall.

A local women's construction company did the labor, and lots of volunteers mounted tiles. We had a big dedication ceremony at which Jesse Jackson spoke, saying he wanted to see the Berlin Wall come down and a Peace Wall take its place. The concept of the wall and of the artist in everyone was very inspiring to people. Someone mentioned to me that they were going to send a press release to TASS, the main News Agency of what was then still the Soviet Union. I said, "Great," figuring nothing would come of it. I felt completely fulfilled just having seen things come this far.

That weekend something else happened that would also change my life. That same weekend of ecstasy, when I was at the highest point of my happiness and joy about my work, I found out that the genetic disorder I had carried in my body since the day I was born was now affecting my eyes. I would never be totally blind, but the

affliction causes progressive dimming of the light, eliminating the ability to perceive detail, both close up and far away. My appointment with destiny had arrived.

A week later someone from TASS called, saying they were coming to California to do a television piece about the wall. The Mayor of Berkeley got involved, flying to Nicaragua to bring back peace tiles painted there. The five-minute television segment made by the TASS crew became the first news feature from California televised throughout the Soviet Union when diplomatic relations were officially reestablished between our two countries in 1988.

One day I got a long distance phone call from a woman who said, "We are coming to California with 100 children. We want to help you build the wall for peace." She was calling from the Soviet Union, and had seen the television program. I arranged 100 American host families, and together the children tiled a wall that, this time, the city gladly supplied. It was at that point, knowing that this work needed to continue, when I began to see that sacrificing myself through all-volunteer time was not going to work. I was still teaching in the Blue Rider School, and having renters kept my expenses low. But I knew I had to earn something more than just enough to cover my expenses. I had to sustain my energy and personal resources. I didn't yet know that the Peace Wall would become my whole life.

In 1989 I was invited by the Soviet Union to live in Moscow to do a peace wall. During the year I was there I worked with 10,000 children in schools and pioneer camps, and we tiled a block-long wall on the Arbat, a twelfth century "mall" near the Kremlin. The Russians, who regard a quote from Dostoyevski as their national motto—"Only beauty will save the world"—embraced the concept of the peace wall with great warmth and eagerness. People would meet my train at 3:00 in the morning, at a five-minute whistle stop, with flowers and good wishes. I was in heaven and wanted to continue this work for the rest of my life.

Inspired by a woman at the Center for Soviet-American Dialogue, which was where I was based, I wrote a letter to the Mayor of Berlin to ask about building a peace wall there. To my amazement, he wrote back. In my mind, the idea of a peace wall around the world started to take root. We would build a circle of love around the earth, like preventative medicine, with sections of it in different communities and different countries.

Although the subsequent Mayor of Berlin was not interested in the wall, back home in 1990, I was ready to create a way in which I could carry on this world wall. A legal firm helped me *pro bono* to create a nonprofit corporation, and they absorbed most of the major fees. In the process of developing a Board of Directors, I began to learn about interdependence and to free myself even further of that outmoded paradigm of the individual artist working alone.

I think it is essential that people recognize what creativity is and use it as a tool in daily life. Every time you make a phone call, it's a creative act. Every choice in how to respond to another person is a creative act. It's so easy to get stuck in the polarities of good/bad, right/wrong, realistic/unrealistic, but you can hold those opposites in the same moment. That is the artistic process, that is peacemaking, and it is available to everyone. To me, being visually impaired and being a visual artist is exactly that same paradox—it is possible for me to be both. And while I accept what life has given me, at the same time I count on miracles.

EILEEN TABATA FITZPATRICK

Kanojo
Irvine, California

Kanojo is more than a company that creates elegant and practical clothing for Asian-American women—it is a vehicle to convey the moving history of Japanese-Americans from ancient times to the present. In a unique method of marketing, Kanojo contributes 10% of all sales to the community organizations that sponsor its fashion show which is presented as a historical pageant. Founders/owners Eileen Tabata Fitzpatrick and her cousin Vicki Yamagami Ragasa have expanded Kanojo from its living room debut in 1990 to its three showrooms in Los Angeles, San Jose and Sacramento—in addition to a mobile presentation. One of Kanojo's creations was invited to be included in a special exhibit in the Smithsonian Institute.

My cousin Vicki and I grew up spending all our spring and summer vacations together. We're two years apart in age and very similar in our tastes. By our late 40s, both of us had enjoyed fulfilling careers, and we both had also reached a turning point in them. One evening over dinner, she and I were reflecting on how as kids we always used to dress our dolls alike. Vicki, who knew how to sew, had made all the outfits for them. In the midst of laughing over our childhood recollections, we remembered how strange we thought it as children that our mothers used to sew all their own clothing. "Why don't you shop in the stores for clothes?" we asked them. They had answered, laughingly, that it was difficult to shop when they couldn't find clothes in the right proportions. "We have to make our clothes because our bodies are different," they said. It was in remembering our mothers' words that Kanojo was conceived.

Vicki and I had grown up to marry, have families and careers. She had become a highly acclaimed fashion designer in Los Angeles, winning national awards for her creations. Climbing the corporate ladder, I had become an executive vice president of a company that assisted school teachers in creating retirement funds. Marketing and communications were my areas of expertise. As fate would have it, twenty years into our respective careers, my cousin and I found ourselves simultaneously unemployed. The company Vicki worked for closed its doors at the peak of its success, and my husband and I decided that our rapidly expanding company had grown up, and it was time for us to do something new with our time and talents.

One day my husband suggested, "You and your cousin are both so interested in your heritage and the struggles Japanese-Americans have faced. Why don't you get together and do something related to that?" Remembering our childhoods that evening at dinner was the spark that set his idea on fire for us. Vicki and I realized that there are a lot of Asian-American women who still, like our mothers, face frustration in finding clothing. Maybe we could pool our skills and respond to those needs. When I told my husband, who is a brilliant financial strategist, he said "I'll back you if you come up with a business concept that makes sense."

Vicki and I figured out what attributes we wanted in our line of clothing. Above all else, we wanted it to fit Asian proportions and to flatter Asian skin tones. We also wanted clothing that would respond to the practical needs of women today whether they were mothers, career women, or retirees. That meant washability, comfort, simplicity. Vicki set to creating the clothing while I worked on how we would market it. We decided we would begin testing the market by inviting people to a show in my home. I made up some little flyers, inviting friends and relatives to our first showing.

People loved it. They bought everything they could get their hands on. Over the next six months, we had lots of home parties. My cousin and two highly skilled Japanese seamstresses produced the clothing in her home. Then I would put on a little show, talking about our mothers and why we were making these clothes. We showed people how to mix and match and how to dress to flatter themselves. As interest grew, we realized that this could indeed be a viable business. My cousin suggested using "she" in Japanese as our name, and Kanojo was born.

I could certainly see that we were filling a need, I could see the eyes light up as women found items made exactly for them—but something was missing for me. Talking about clothing had become a struggle. I love public speaking, so this was very unusual. I began to realize that for twenty years I had been working in a business that had a fulfilling and enriching social mission. That's what Kanojo needed. Clothing alone felt so inanimate to me. Kanojo needed a heartbeat.

A sudden wave of memory came back to me of something that my father had said when I was a child. My parents had been among the 120,000 Japanese Americans who were confined in concentration camps in the Southwest during World War II. My father and mother met there, and that is where I was born. I remembered my father explaining to me, when I was about eight years old, that we hadn't done anything wrong, that what had happened was very unjust, but that the best thing to do was not look back in bitterness but go on and achieve things in life. He told me that my Japanese heritage is a very beautiful one and that I should have pride in it. "Ours is a culture that will live on only if you talk about it and preserve it with pride," he had said. "Maybe someday you will find an opportunity to give back to your own Japanese American community."

As a child, I didn't know why he was telling me those things. I do remember that after the camps, when we had come back to the west coast, we lived in an area where there were a lot of army families. Many of the men had served in the Pacific during the war. I

remember brutal attacks by other children in grade school, being called "dirty Jap" and other names. At night I would cry and wonder, "Why did I have to be born this way? What's wrong with me?" I didn't like being Japanese-American. My parents, like most others who shared the internment experience, had submerged their feelings, and we children didn't really know that they had lost everything, including their pride. It wasn't until college, when I and many others in my generation did research and went back to ask our parents for the real story, that we began to rewrite history to tell the truth.

Now, at the birth of Kanojo, I realized that my father was talking about having a mission, having a way to enhance and support our Japanese-American community. I knew that scout groups, senior citizens organizations, church groups were all struggling to raise funds. Why not figure out a way to support them through Kanojo? This would make it purposeful. This would give it heart. We could present our fashion show, as we had been doing in homes, for Japanese-American service organizations and then give our hosts 10% of our sales. We asked at one of our house parties if anyone knew of a group that needed a fundraiser, and we began with a well-known Japanese women's group in San Jose.

At that first show, all my passion about my heritage arose, and my presentation, which was supposed to be short and sweet, turned into a philosophical statement about our people. I could see in the teary eyes and glowing faces that I was really touching a chord. So piece by piece over time, the show grew to tell the story of the evolution of our Japanese-American culture from its origins in Japan in ancient samurai times, through the Japanese migration to America, to the point where we have become a part of the American fabric. Eventually, as I added period music to go with it, and then period costumes and replicas of ancient props, my narrative story became a passionately woven tale depicting the true evolutionary struggle of my people. The portrayal went from being a fashion show to being a "Celebration of the Japanese-American cultural experience" in the form of a three-act play.

I have found that in order to portray the story accurately, it has been important for the actors to come from the Asian communities where we are making our presentation. So before each show, I request a cadre of inexperienced volunteers from the sponsoring group to play the parts. In each segment of the story, these models wear ancient costumes or Kanojo-created fashions to visually convey each passing chapter of our history from the 1800s to the late 1900s. My cousin Vicki has cleverly combined the ancient fabrics of the past with modern day fabrics and fashion stylings to show how our culture has evolved while stubbornly maintaining, as evidenced in the fluid lines of Kanojo fashions, the original flavor of the ancient kimono, our native costume, and the robes of the samurai lords. In essence, everything and nothing has changed over time. Only someone with Vicki's depth of personal experience in understanding the struggle our people have come through could create clothing with such an innate Japanese feeling.

After each celebratory performance before large audiences of appreciative Asians and non-Asians, the sponsoring group asks the guests to take a ten-minute break while Kanojo's staff and the sponsoring team literally convert the performance room into a lovely shopping boutique. The audience then returns, motivated and uplifted by the show, to begin shopping for fashions depicted in the show. They feel exhilarated not only in being able to select an exciting piece from the show but also in knowing that a portion of their purchase is contributed to the sponsoring entity, and that they are taking home a bit of their heritage. In essence, the experience is a truly positive one for everyone—the sponsor, the guests, and for Kanojo.

The business has demanded a great deal from Vicki and me—maintaining the schedule of shows, designing the clothing, and manufacturing no more than a select quantity of each item. But I feel that Kanojo was meant to be. As our mission statement says, "The opportunity to make a difference in the lives of others is available to all who enter this life." I feel that Kanojo is our particular mission, instilling pride in people old and young, as they witness the passage of history and see that, after all of it, we live on.

SUSAN LEVY

Femi-9 Contracting Corporation
Lindenhurst, New York

On the letterhead of Susan Levy's business, a filigreed border frames the sil-

houette of a pavement milling machine used in highway construction. This is

the logo for Femi-9 (word play intended) Contracting Corporation. Founder

and Owner Susan Levy is a Certified Construction Associate (CCA) who

not only runs the company but works on site alongside her employees, build-

ing and repairing federal, state and municipal roads and highways in the

tri-state area of New York, Connecticut, and New Jersey. An award-winning

businesswoman, she served in 1996 as President of the National Association

of Women in Construction (NAWIC), an international organization for

women employed in all facets of the construction industry.

Never in my wildest imagination would I have thought that one day I would be a business owner. If you had asked me when I graduated from high school in 1967 what I would be doing fifteen or twenty years down the road, I probably would have answered that I'd be home raising children as a wife and mother. Instead, at a time when women in the field of contracting and construction were few and far between, I started Femi-9.

I was probably drawn to non-traditional roles for women because I was raised as the only girl with five brothers. I had also joined the U.S. Army at a time when far fewer women were in the military. It seemed a better option after high school than trying to work and go to college at the same time. During the two years that I served I gained a lot of self-confidence. Since I worked primarily in administrative positions as a secretary, I assumed that's what I would continue doing when I got out. I felt that anything within that realm suited me.

After college courses in business and accounting, I found an office job at a company where I knew I could move up. They leased heavy equipment to contractors. Over the years, I learned as much as I could about the equipment and the business, and I continued getting promotions.

By the time I reached the position of Vice-President of Finance and Administration, I began thinking that, although I was very happy at work, I had probably reached the highest position the company could ever offer. I had a settlement, just sitting in the bank, from a car accident I'd had not long before. I could use it to start a company of my own. If it didn't work out, I 'd have something to fall back on until I could find another position. This was my opportunity. I was either going to do something on my own or work for somebody else for the rest of my life.

I wasn't really sure what I wanted to do—maybe open a little gift shop. The more I thought about it, however, the more I realized I was very comfortable working with contractors. And I had noticed something over the years—most of the time when contractors called to find out whether we had a piece of equipment called a concrete saw, they often would ask, "Do you have someone to run it for us?" There didn't seem to be anyone doing specifically that kind of work. Maybe there was an opportunity in that. Perhaps it was a niche I could fill.

For the next year and a half, I did some informal research and discovered that there was indeed a big demand in the area for contractors who could do that kind of highway and road construction. I decided to take the plunge. I went home and told my husband what I'd been thinking. I had done the research, I had the money in hand, it was now or never. He said, "It's not always easy to start your own business. If that's what you want to do, go for it. I'm behind you 100%." And he has been. In fact, now that he has retired, he works for my company.

His response was a great relief to me, because if he had said, "I don't think it's a good idea; you won't be able to pull it off and you'll lose your money," I might have had second thoughts, and maybe I wouldn't have done it. Of course I probably wouldn't have married someone who thought like that. According to my way of thinking back then, my responsibility was to my family—my husband and two stepchildren. I couldn't have done it if they weren't supportive.

As soon as I was free, I started doing research to learn what equipment I needed to get started. There is a tremendous selection of concrete saws and blades for every possible combination of pavement—gravel, old concrete, new concrete, asphalt. I had to know which blades and which sizes to use for different applications. I toured a diamond blade manufacturing plant in Texas. I read a lot of literature from various manufacturers, and I asked a lot of questions.

I found a small space to rent and a bank I could work with. I wasn't new to the financial world because of my former position, but it was a giant step to be talking to bankers for my own company instead of someone else's. I was very proud to be carving out a place for myself in a non-traditional field, and I wanted to have a name and a feminine-looking logo that would let people know there was a woman at the helm. Names like Petticoat Construction and Ms. Contracting had already been taken. My lawyer suggested Femi-Nine. I liked it, but decided to use the numeral instead of spelling it out, and that was it.

I located a young man who was familiar with operating a concrete saw and asked him if he was willing to come on board at a new company. My main concern was how he would feel working for a woman. That didn't seem to make much difference to him; and if the business didn't work out, he assured me, he could always find something else.

I sent a mass mailing to all of the construction companies in the area and made a lot of personal phone calls to people I knew working in them. I wrote up promotional materials to send out when people called. Then I waited for clients to show up. That was probably the biggest challenge. It took a lot of patience. People weren't just jumping on the bandwagon and saying, "Oh, Susan Levy has started her own company. Let's give her the job." My first year in business I probably didn't gross more than $50,000—enough to keep the payroll going, buy some equipment and plod along. Fortunately I didn't need to draw a salary every week in order to support my family. It was harder without my regular income, but we all tightened our belts for a while. I knew if I could just hang in there long enough, I would have a thriving business. I questioned at times, however, whether or not I was capable of that level of patience.

Shortly after starting the business, I began an accredited, five-year home study program in construction management, offered through the NAWIC Education Foundation. I chose home study because it afforded me an opportunity to learn more about construction, without taking valuable time away from my new business. I am quite proud of the fact that I completed the program within one year, the first person ever to do so!

Femi-9's first job came from one of the largest construction companies on Long Island, and I still do business with them today. I like to think they gave me the job because the price was right, not because they knew me. But certainly we have continued to do business with them because I showed them that I am capable.

When I first opened my business, I wasn't always taken seriously as the owner of a contracting company. When someone called to get a bid on a job, they would typically assume that they were going to be speaking to a man. So sometimes what I would get is, "Hi, honey, can I talk to one of the boys?" I found it very annoying that anyone could call whoever was on the other end of the phone, whether an estimator or a secretary, "honey." In my book that is a term of endearment and thus limited in its use. It still comes up these days, but to a much lesser degree. I've come to answer, "There's only one person who can call me honey, and that's my husband. Now how can I help you?"

Another typical call would be: "Hi, honey, let me have one of the estimators." The conversation would go something like: "Yes, can I help you?" "Well, I don't want to have to explain it twice. If you'd just let me talk to one of the estimators. . . ." "You're talking to the estimator." As they would proceed to relate the details of the job, it would be clear that I was going to have to prove my abilities.

Some of that attitude was due to the fact that there were companies that took advantage of the federal affirmative action programs by setting up wives, mothers or sisters as titular owners who in fact knew nothing about the business. I had to break through that assumption as well as traditional stereotypes to let people know that this was a legitimate business and that I, a woman, was the *working* owner. I was up against attitudes that had been around for many, many years, and it took stamina and perseverance to get past them. I knew that over time people would get to know me and the quality of my work. They had to see me on the job site, getting my hands dirty just like everybody else.

And I do. My trade affiliation is with the Teamsters Union, and often I am one of the truck drivers on a site. Especially in the early, formative years, it was not uncommon for me to come in at four-thirty or five o'clock in the morning to do paper work, go out and spend all day on-site, then return at 4:30 in the afternoon to spend another hour or so answering phone calls and taking care of work that had accumulated during the day.

As far as I'm concerned, when I'm out on-site, I'm just one of the workers. I've never experienced sexual harassment, but often there's a lot of profanity. When I'm around, the guys will stop and say, "Whoops, excuse me." My standard answer is, "I didn't hear anything." It's not really an issue for me, but I'm of two minds about it. On the one hand, I certainly want to be treated as an equal, and on the other hand, I sure wish sometimes that they'd clean up their act!

Those of us working in an industry that is non-traditional for women have a very important role to play. We are paving the way for future generations of women to come along and equal or better our success. NAWIC has started national programs to introduce in schools the idea of a career in construction. One of our most successful is the Block Kids Building Competition for elementary school children, which I was instrumental in developing. Through programs such as this, we've been very successful in overcoming some of the stereotypes that people hold about construction. I like to show that this is a viable option for women. When I go out to speak to groups of young women, I like to tell them, "Some day you can even own your own company."

SUSAN DAVIS

Capital Missions Company
West Chicago, Illinois

Convinced that most business leaders really do want to make a positive difference for society and the environment, Susan Davis started a company that creates networks of business leaders who support and inspire each other in solving social problems. "When you give business leaders a chance to meet and interact with others like themselves who also have higher values," she reports, "they take advantage of the opportunity." The slogan on her business card clearly defines her mission and her clientele as "Companies Doing Well by Doing Good." Susan is currently writing a book about her experiences in starting business leadership networks and about how people can create similar personal networks for themselves, comprised of "kindred spirits," people who share your values and your desires to make a difference in the world.

As my 50th birthday was approaching, I felt a strong urge to clarify what my special expertise was, the unique contribution I could make with my life. I'd never had the opportunity to take a long vacation, and I decided that this was the time. I made arrangements to have my children cared for and went to Hawaii for an entire month. I spent the time walking, swimming, reading, thinking, writing. I thought about my life and what was important to me. I gave myself permission to fulfill my destiny, whatever that was supposed to be.

I grew up with a mother who was a volunteer and a dad who was a highly ethical businessman. Both had very satisfying lives, and I wanted to combine their experiences in what I did with my life. Encouraging socially responsible business was the way I found to do that. As soon as I graduated from college, I began helping to start companies that solved social problems. Later, I branched into creating business leadership networks. I started The Committee of 200, a network of businesswomen with multi-million-dollar companies who wanted to be supportive of each other in modeling entrepreneurship. That was the first national network of business leaders I created, and I could see that it was profoundly transformational for those involved.

When I took a position at the Harris Bank in Chicago, I used that first network as a model and created other networks for groups with particular financial issues. My heart was still in socially responsible business, rather than finances per se, but I was divorced and had two young children to raise. I had been at the Harris Bank for nine years by the time I went to Hawaii. I knew that if I was ever going to get back into socially responsible business, now was the time. I made myself a promise that sometime during my fiftieth year, I was either going to get involved in social responsibility at the bank, or leave and do it on my own.

I designed an initiative for socially responsible investing at the bank. However, before it could be implemented, the bank went through a huge downsizing. Clearly it wasn't the right time for my proposal. That left me with one option if I was to keep my promise to myself.

In June of 1990 I left the bank to start my own company. During thirty years of very tough, challenging experiences, I had developed techniques to help business leaders use networks to maximize positive social impact. I had probably made every mistake that could be made and learned from them. Now was the time to run my own business. I had waited until I was ready. Capital Missions would be an expression of my own deepest beliefs, hopes and dreams. It would be my own unique contribution.

The time was right for another reason as well. I believe in family first, and to me it would have been putting my kids at risk to start my own business much before I did. Moving in high-powered business circles for quite a few years had been grueling enough, even with excellent live-in housekeepers. Now that my children

were ten and thirteen, they still needed my time and attention, but to a different degree than when they were younger.

I didn't know exactly what my business would be. So, after leaving the bank, I intended to spend the first three months planning. I got a really good designer to do a beautiful logo that I thought symbolized the ethics and values of my company. I wanted to be located downtown and found a space—two rooms decorated in a nurturing and attractive way—in a temporary employment agency run by two successful women. I found another woman who owned a public relations firm and shared my values, and we put out a press release saying I would be doing consulting in the field of socially responsible business. Many articles about the opening of Capital Missions appeared, including, to the delight and amazement of my friends, a five-column story in *The Chicago Tribune*.

I also sent out a letter to several hundred people I considered friends, telling them what I was doing with my life and asking that they "take a moment to sit back and send a blessing up to the Universe that Capital Missions is launched." That blessing really must have worked, because never in the five years since I've started the company have I had to go out after new business. It has always come to me.

In fact, I never did have time to do a marketing plan. The first week I was open, two people showed up and each took half my consulting time for a year—and both of them asked me to do exactly what I love to do, create business leadership networks! One wanted a network of socially responsible investors, and the other wanted a network for key influencers in sustainable agriculture. So from the day I opened the doors of my company, I felt secure.

My whole life has been about this kind of synchronicity. I believe that higher forces are at work and that if we just stick to our values, things work out fine. I have deep faith in that. I have developed a philosophy of "Trust the Universe." Things materialize when they're needed—and sometimes even before. For example, usually it's very hard for entrepreneurs to raise money, but money just came to me. A few years after Capital Missions had gotten off the ground, a friend asked if I wanted an investor, because he knew someone who was interested in my business. I didn't have any immediate plans for expansion, but the values of the potential investor matched mine as closely as anyone's could. So I accepted the money and put it in the bank for a year until I decided exactly how I wanted to expand. At that point, I brought someone in to share the CEO spot with me and used the funds to finance that.

When I started Capital Missions, I felt that it was my destiny. I used to be anxious, questioning whether I was doing what I was supposed to do with my life. But looking back now I can see that all my experiences have exactly prepared me to do this work. That perception has led to a great deal of joy. When you finally find the reason why you're here, it's an ecstatic experience, and it continues to be for me.

SARAHN HENDERSON

Mother's Keeper
Atlanta, Georgia

While working as a birth attendant, Sarahn Henderson saw how urgently

mothers need help at home after childbirth, and she created a postpartum

doula service in response. The ancient Greek term doula, *"one who serves a*

woman," has currently come to mean "mothering the mother" and refers to

women who are specifically trained to provide support to mothers before,

during and after childbirth. Mother's Keeper trains and employs postpar-

tum doulas. Sarahn is also a childbirth educator and is writing a book on

traditional midwifery and childbirth practices with an Africentric focus.

When my first baby was six months old, the midwife who had attended his birth invited me to be with her during her own homebirth. I felt honored and during her labor did what I could to help her feel more comfortable. Some hours after her baby was born, she said, "Come over here and sit down." I sat next to her on the bed, she took my hand and said to me, "You have the hands of a midwife."

It all unfolded from there. I began attending home births as a labor assistant. It wasn't long before I realized that a lot of moms were at home by themselves with their newborns. They didn't always know what they were supposed to do to take care of the babies or themselves. During this period when a mother should be recovering, many were also managing their homes. Although I'd had some help from my husband, family, and friends after each of my five children were born, I knew what it was like to have a new baby with nobody around during the day to help or give emotional support.

Being a community resource person, I started arranging for women I knew to join me as volunteers in helping new mothers. But it was a big commitment for many of them to take on. I also realized that you really have to be born a nurturer, and not everyone is. So I decided to develop a postpartum program in order to fill the need I saw and to create some extra income for my family.

I sat down and wrote out everything that would be included in my service. I would go to women's homes during the daytime for the first week or two after a birth, to nurture mothers and help them gain confidence and security in getting to know their new babies. I would counsel them on holding the baby, changing diapers, breastfeeding, treating the umbilical cord and jaundice—all these things you need to know about infants. I would give the mother massages and make sure she was eating well and resting. If there were other children, I would feed them and get them to school. And I'd do the other essential tasks, like shopping, cleaning up, and doing the laundry.

A friend of mine came up with the name "Mother's Keeper." It sounded so sweet to me when I heard it. For the logo on my brochure, I had an image in mind of a woman holding a baby in her arms. A friend helped me put it all together and took it to her office to print it out on her computer.

I passed brochures out to friends who were midwives, to other childbirth instructors, and to prenatal exercise teachers. I also wanted to distribute them through the offices of obstetricians. For me, that was the real challenge. I had a picture of them as being *the* professionals, and the kind of nonmedical service I was proposing had rarely been heard of, at least in Georgia. Could I present myself in such a manner that they would accept my service and want to promote it themselves?

First of all, I knew I had to dress the part, so I went to my sister, and she gave me some suits she had outgrown and had been keeping in the back of her closet for just such moments. The next hurdle would be getting past the receptionists. I knew I would have to explain to them who I was and what I had come to present. That felt harder to do than talking to the doctors themselves!

The first office I chose to go to was one with a nurse midwife on the medical team. I knew she would probably be more receptive to this idea than the male physicians. When my scheduled time to talk with the team arrived, I felt nervous and scared. But I found that once I started telling them about what I do and the benefits of postpartum care, I started feeling fine. At first it was hard for the doctors to acknowledge that there were extended needs after delivery and after the hospital. The nurse midwife started to recount what it was like after she had come home with a new baby and didn't have any help. By the end of the conversation, they had decided to give it a try and asked me to leave some brochures in the office.

A lot of my work in getting my business going has been in educating doctors and educating mothers. I believe in letting mothers discover their own maternal instincts. I don't take over the care of her baby, rather I support the mother in caring for her baby—and for herself. Some of my clients are professionals who were used to eating dinner out every night before they had a baby. I tell them, "When I come here, I don't cook out of boxes and packages and cans. Everything I prepare is fresh." I try to show them that this is the way they need to eat, especially if they are going to provide their child's nutrients through their breast milk.

I think it is in my blood to have this ability to teach. People in my family all the way back to my great grandmother have been teachers. But even when I went into early childhood education in college, I knew that I wasn't going to follow them into the public school system. I didn't know what I was going to be doing or how, but I knew it was going to be different. I think I am the only woman

in my family who has started and maintained a business. My father is an entrepreneur, and I think that has given me the confidence to do something other than punching in on a 9 to 5 schedule. Sometimes as my mother watched me struggle, she tried to encourage me to get a job that would provide a steady income. Resisting that temptation was one of my biggest challenges.

I came to the point a couple of years ago when I had to make a decision about whether I wanted to make Mother's Keeper into a business that really worked or let it casually go on like just another thing I do. The turning point happened on a trip I took to Africa. I was going to Ghana to capture the stories of midwives and moms for my book on childbirth practices. It turned out that all the people I traveled with were entrepreneurs. They kept feeding me with success stories of their own businesses and talking to me about where I could take Mother's Keeper if I wanted to make a greater commitment to it.

What I found most inspiring about them was the self-satisfaction they had in knowing that there was a purpose in their lives and that they were accomplishing it. That renewed something in me. I knew that my purpose in life is to serve in the nurturing and the care of mothers as well as babies. But I had to ask myself if I was willing to put in the overtime it would take to make Mothers' Keeper grow into a business that could make that care available to many women. I would have to incorporate it, get it insured and bonded, and then start developing it into an agency and training other people. Was I ready to make the extra sacrifices it would take? But I knew I wanted to show my children, especially the two in high school, that they could be successful if they applied themselves. And I wanted to see where my potential lay. So I said, "Okay, let's take it a step further and see where it takes us."

Right now I have two women working with me. For their training I've brought in a lactation consultant, a pediatrician, and a woman who does infant massage, and I teach them ethics and how to conduct themselves in this work. My next challenge is to try to get insurance companies to reimburse families for postpartum services. My main clients are families that can afford the service. My ultimate goal is to get Medicaid to cover this so that I'll be addressing people, such as teenagers and single mothers, who really need the help so they can get a good start in parenting and give their babies a good start in life.

All along, in doing Mothers' Keeper, the doors have just opened wide, as if it was pre-destined for me. And as Mother's Keeper has grown, I have grown also. I like to say that my work in assisting labor is my calling, education is my profession, and through both of them has come Mother's Keeper.

KRISTI COWLES

Pederson Victorian Bed & Breakfast
Singing Wolf Center
Lake Geneva, Wisconsin

Located in the rural Lake Geneva retreat and recreation area in southeast-

ern Wisconsin, the Pederson Victorian is a ten-room Queen Anne built in

1880 which Kristi Cowles has converted into her four-room bed and break-

fast. She features full, vegetarian breakfasts served in her formal din-

ingroom and lists among amenities the absence of televisions, whirlpools,

and bedside telephones. To top off her dream, the main room of the Victorian

is the site of her Singing Wolf Center which hosts workshops with thinkers

and doers on the leading edge of cultural change.

The idea of a bed and breakfast had been with me for years, and I guess it just kept knocking and knocking until I listened. Actually, it all began with PeeWee Peterson. She was my high school idol in Wittenberg, Wisconsin, a quaint little town of 872 people. PeeWee was a senior, and I was a freshman. For some reason she took me and my best friend under her wing, carted us around in her car, and generally made us feel like we were important. One time, many years later, when I was home for Christmas, my mother said, "Guess what PeeWee Peterson is doing? She has a bed and breakfast out on Nantucket Island." That was one of those snap moments of recognition for me.

All my life there have been times when I have known in an instant some major step I would take. That moment of insight sets into motion a sequence of thinking and planning, but they continually refer back to that dramatic intuition when I *knew* without question. That morning at my mother's house I knew that someday, somehow, I would have my own bed and breakfast.

However, I settled into sixteen years of marriage and children in southeastern Wisconsin, and developed a career as a singer — jazz, old and new Broadway, some pop. My keyboardist and I

played only in local clubs and hotels, so I could get home at night. When my husband and I divorced, I continued singing—seventeen years in all—to support myself and my two daughters. Eventually that also paid the way for the three of us to go through college.

When my girls were grown and I left for graduate school in San Francisco, everyone said I would never come back to the Midwest. I loved San Francisco and decided that after I received my Masters in East/West Psychology, I would stay on at least another year to do more training. The idea of the bed and breakfast had not left me, but I had no idea how I might carry it out. I knew I wanted to use the skills I was learning in my psychology program, and I didn't see how the two ideas fit together.

The last quarter before graduation, I began feeling stuck, and I wasn't sure why, so I decided to spend a day at home meditating and being quiet. Halfway through the day, suddenly a vivid image of a beautiful Victorian house dropped into my mind. It was almost as if I were walking through it. There was a big kitchen and a large carpeted main room. I knew immediately it was a bed and break-fast, and that it was mine. Since San Francisco is known for its many fine Victorians, the thought passed through my mind that I would find my place there. But surrounding the house in my vision were the rolling hills of Wisconsin—I saw home. I knew I was going back. I knew what I wanted to do—the place I had seen was not just a B&B. That big room was a place for classes. I realized that I did not have to choose between doing the bed and breakfast or doing something with my graduate work. I would locate in the bed and breakfast itself a center in which to offer workshops for personal and cultural change. I would invite others to teach, and I would teach there myself.

It took me six months to get settled in Wisconsin and recover from the previous years of graduate school and full-time work.

I knew it was only a matter of time before I found the place I had seen in my vision. One day when I finally felt ready to move on, I called a realtor and said, "Give me your listings on everything for sale that's Victorian in southeastern Wisconsin." I took the print-outs and starting driving around. I looked at six or seven from the outside only and drove on. I knew what I was looking for. Late that afternoon, I stopped in to see a good friend of mine and asked if she would come with me to see three more in the Lake Geneva area. When we pulled up in front of the Pederson Victorian that late July afternoon, there it was. It looked exactly like the house I had seen in my vision.

The place was in good shape, although I would have to do some work to bring it up to code. And I could bear the decor until later when I could redecorate room by room. The location was great. We were no more than an hour and half from four good-sized cities, including Chicago, in an area that already attracted a lot of people for rest and recreation. The only equity I had was the condominium I had bought in Milwaukee after my divorce, so I found a very small, old bank and convinced the president that I was a good risk. He had lived in that city forever and knew what a stubborn, conservative, industrial town it was. I said, "If I could make my living for seventeen years in this area singing—when musicians far better than I am couldn't—then don't you think I can do this? He agreed. Just before I left, I said, "Okay, now I have a philosophical question for you. In a case like mine, when it comes down to it, how much do you rely on your intuition?" This man had been in the business for about forty years. He looked at me with a twinkle in his eye and answered, "About a hundred percent."

I got both businesses going almost simultaneously. The bed and breakfast opened its doors in January 1990, and the Singing Wolf

Center followed a few months later, opening with two Sunday afternoon workshops taught by me and a local friend.

I named each of the four bedrooms in the bed and breakfast after my grandmothers and great-grandmothers—Myrtle Amanda Jorgenson, Anna Serena Hanson, Jenny Medora Williams, and Hega Johnson. My mother has researched her Norwegian lineage all the way back to the 16th century, and I feel a deep connection to my ancestors. When I was growing up, both sets of my grandparents lived nearby, and my sister and I spent almost as much time with them as we did with our own parents. In fact, we learned how to read well before kindergarten, sitting on the laps of the eighth-graders in the one-room schoolhouse where Grandma Myrtle taught. I consider her work very entrepreneurial for her time and think that it is partly her pioneering spirit that accounts for my style.

Pederson Victorian, out of the 273 Bed & Breakfasts in the state, is the only one with a visible focus on a concern for the earth and the environment. My goal, for instance, is to have all our linens be 100% cotton. Most of them are antiques with lace and good thick cotton which I found at estate sales. I decided to minimize technology and so all year long, including when it is freezing in winter, I hang sheets, pillowcases, and towels on the clothesline to dry—just like my mother and grandmother did before me. All paper products are recycled, I use no chemicals and buy nothing from factory farms. My breakfasts are vegetarian and so savory they've been written up in several newspapers. At first I didn't publicize these differences, but I get bolder and bolder as I get older and older! My marketing niche is narrow, however I have learned how to find the people who are looking for what I offer.

The same is true of the Singing Wolf Center. Rarely have I had to cancel a workshop due to lack of enrollment. Some local people attend, but most participants are from out of town. When the leader is well-known, people often come from very far away. When there is room, they stay in my bed and breakfast.

So both of my dreams have merged, which is very satisfying, although it's not always easy. My biggest challenge has been getting past my fear. To follow this dream was the biggest leap I had ever taken. Often I moved ahead despite the terror in the pit of my stomach. Even when nothing seemed to be happening, I went on, believing that things would work out. There have been times when my house payment would be due the next day, and I had nothing to pay it with. And then checks would arrive in the mail, sometimes as a contribution, most of the time as unexpected business, reservations for the B&B or for a workshop down the line.

Some people looking at my books might say, "You're not successful," but how do you measure and define abundance? I have a life rich with guests, friends and family, work and play. I live in my bed and breakfast under towering old maple and walnut trees, in the rolling hills of southeastern Wisconsin. I teach and host wonderful and interesting people at the Singing Wolf Center. To me, that's wealth. It all sprang from that defining vision I had one quiet day—after that, everything came together like a weaving. And now, in fact, one of my favorite classes to teach is the one about creativity and following intuition.

GAYLE McENROE

Metal Service Inc.
St. Paul, Minnesota

Gayle McEnroe is one of a handful of women in the nation who owns a

business in the highly competitive, traditionally male-dominated field of

wholesale metals distribution. Metal Service Inc. provides stainless steel,

aluminum and carbon steel in tubing, rods and sheets to manufacturing

companies for products ranging from lawn furniture to escalators to light

rail transit vehicles. A member of the Pembina Band of the Ojibwe Tribe,

Gayle also serves on the board of the Minnesota American Indian Chamber

of Commerce.

Whenever I give talks to young people, I explain how important it is to do their very best at every job they have, because they don't know how the cards are going to be shuffled, how someone they work for now might affect their lives later. How could I have imagined then, when I was 21 working at my first job in the metals industry that the remainder of my life would be so profoundly affected by my boss? Many years later, he came back into my life as what I would call my first "angel," and made it possible for me to start Metal Service Inc. I believe that came about because right from the beginning I began to establish my credibility as a reliable, dependable person with high integrity who delivers on what she says.

I began my career fresh out of business school. I was a single mom with a three-year-old child. I hadn't finished high school myself, and my one desire was to see my daughter make it through. For that I needed a good job. Because I had taken college preparatory classes when I was in high school, I didn't have any skills that could immediately earn me an adequate wage. Instead of getting stuck in jobs as an unskilled laborer, I decided to go to business school to learn accounting and office skills. I enrolled my daughter in a great Headstart program and set out to change my life.

About three weeks before graduation, a company with a job opening called the school looking for a man who could type. In those days you could make that kind of gender-specific request. I got on the phone and asked why they needed a man for the job? I was told that the company was in the metals industry and women just hadn't worked out for them. I asked, "Well, do you have to lift the metal?" When the answer was no, I suggested I come in for an interview. I got the job. It was at a small company with three employees. I was what used to be called a Gal Friday, which meant I did everything, including opening the office in the morning, getting bottled water, typing, accounting, and answering phones. When the salesperson got busy, I began helping customers myself. I gravitated naturally in that direction because I already had a background in sales—although not a typical one.

When I was growing up, a man used to come to our neighborhood with household wares—fly swatters, spatulas, vases—which the kids would peddle to local housewives to earn five cents on every dollar. At the age of five, I began doing door-to-door sales. Of course I was successful at it; how could I not be? When someone answers a knock on the door and there stands a little girl with a suitcase of goods, they're going to find something to buy. When I was around ten years old, I figured out where our supplier was buying his goods, and I started buying and selling on my own. At thirteen, I became the youngest Tupperware dealer in the nation, and I was extremely successful at it. Of course part of my success may have been due to the novelty of such a young salesperson, but in my perception, I was successful because I was good at what I was doing. Those early experiences really built my confidence and

self-esteem. We're all given certain skills and talents, and apparently the ability to sell is one of my gifts. This became a great benefit to me in my job at the metals company.

Soon customers were asking to work with me. Three months after I started there, I was asked to find someone else to do the clerical job, and I was promoted to sales. For the next thirteen years, I worked for various firms in the metals industry. When an out-of-state company asked me to establish a branch for them in Minnesota, I accepted. Without knowing it at the time, this process of finding a location, setting up an office, and making contacts with clients was a dress rehearsal for my own business. The search for that branch location caused me to be re-united with my very first boss in the industry, who had since gone into real estate. We hadn't been in contact for years, but he remembered me and offered me a place for the branch in a building he owned.

In 1988 after two successful years, the home office decided to move the branch to the suburbs. I had reached the glass ceiling in that organization and chose not to move with them.

That's when my first angel revealed himself. I was approached by our landlord, my old boss, with an offer. Soon he would have an empty 5,000-square-foot building with an overhead crane. He said, "Why don't you take this space and do something for yourself?" It had previously rented for $2,400 a month. He knew I could go in there and put a business together—he had just seen me do that— and he offered to rent the place to me for $1,000 a month. He gave me a $3,000 loan to set up, and joined me as a 49% silent partner. I was able immediately to get a customer who paid up front for a very large order, and Metal Service Inc. was up and running. About four months later, this same angel lent the business $25,000 and co-signed for an equal amount at the bank so the business could grow.

After a year and a half, I bought him out and, on a handshake, agreed to give him another $16,000 if I was still in business four years later—which I honored when the time came.

I do believe that many potential angels are out there, but you have to earn their respect. This man wasn't acting as a venture capitalist, lending money for a huge return. Nor was he just giving money away, like a philanthropist. We both got something out of it. I got the opportunity to start my own business. He was able to rent a vacant building by helping me to develop a thriving business. I'm sure he enjoyed watching me meet the challenges he had gone through himself at one time in the business. That's what I would call a legitimate angel.

I had been given the opportunity to begin, but my company had to prove itself in order to continue. I like to say that Service is our middle name; that's what I've built the business on, filling orders as quickly as possible, sometimes on weekends or evenings, to build customer satisfaction. That credibility I had begun establishing at 21 years of age continued to grow, and when I went to apply for credit lines, I could offer a hundred references. I had also put in my time, having worked fifteen years in the industry before starting my business. I knew the pros and cons and was very well networked within it. As in any business, it took two or three years before we started making money, but our sales have continually gone up, from $600,000 the first year to $3.4 million by the fourth.

I think the success of a business depends upon having the ability to play the hand that's been dealt you. There are always unexpected circumstances or challenges—like when an order sat in the warehouse for months while one of our clients was in the process of being purchased by another firm, or when some consultants accidentally erased all accounting data from our computer's hard disk.

These required from me the kind of creative thinking that I learned from my father and the resilience and resourcefulness I learned from my mother.

It also took that creativity and resourcefulness when my second child was born not quite three years into the business. I had re-married several years before, and our baby was due during a critical point in the development of the company. The key person couldn't simply take time off, so I purchased a mobile home and parked it about fifty feet from the door of my office. After the baby was born, she stayed in the trailer during the day in the care of her grandmothers, both of whom were willing to help, and I could see her and nurse her. We kept that arrangement until she was nine months old.

My husband works with me now and has always been supportive. I know personally how true it is that a major criterion for success in business is the support of a spouse. My youngest daughter at five years exhibits an interest in business which I try to encourage. My oldest daughter did indeed graduate from high school, and also from a four-year college with a nursing degree. I have started a second business, under the wings of my second angel. And it all started out with my being reliable and making good on my word at my first job when I was 21.

TAMI SIMON

Sounds True Catalog
Boulder, Colorado

Tami Simon creates, produces and distributes original audio tapes of some

of the best thinkers, teachers, and musicians on the leading edge of alterna-

tive health practices, psychological and spiritual growth, and social change.

Since starting out in 1985 as a conference-recording and tape-duplication

service, Sounds True has made the INC 500's list as one of the fastest grow-

ing privately-held companies two years in a row. Sounds True's unique

Prison Audio Project invites customers to donate their listened-to tapes for

distribution to the nation's 1.5 million prisoners.

entered Swarthmore as a philosophy major, wanting to understand the meaning of life. It didn't take long to realize that the academic approach was not going to supply answers. But in my sophomore year, I took classes in Buddhism taught by a professor from Sri Lanka. Nothing I had come upon in the western traditions offered me such a logical explanation of the world and the purpose of human life. Instead of returning to school, I left for the East, traveling for a year through Sri Lanka, India and Nepal to explore meditation practices.

Back in the States, I got a job as a waitress in Boulder, Colorado, where an institute of Buddhist studies was located. In my parents' eyes, by dropping out of college, I had stepped off track. My father said to me, "Tami, that graduation is your ticket to the rest of your life. To your career, to everything." But I knew there was something in me that was going a different way, although I didn't understand why. I knew only that it felt like I had been on a train going 100 miles an hour, and I had just jumped off.

I had been positioned by my formal education to make a significant contribution to the world, and now I had no idea what to do or how to do it. I felt ashamed to be so lost, and I was hungry to use my talents. I decided to volunteer at the local community radio station in Boulder. I had done radio in college and loved it. I had two music programs and an interview show on which I talked to various teachers of spirituality and psychology who passed through town on the lecture circuit. Often I would record their talks and seminars and broadcast them or use excerpts on my show. It was fun and a way to continue the kind of education that meant something to me.

However, despite the opportunities to learn what I was deeply interested in, I felt extremely depressed. I quit my waitress job and tried working at the Boulder Emergency Shelter, thinking perhaps some kind of social work might be a way I could contribute. But I found I didn't really have the patience to do that kind of work. My mother says that I always had so much energy, I was like a tiger looking for something to sink my teeth into. I started praying, "God, I am willing to do your work. Show me what it is. I will do anything. Just show me." I literally said that prayer every day for three months, and then I got an answer.

My father had died when I was 21 and left me a small inheritance. Unsure what to do with it, I decided to go for advice to Jirka Ryssavy, one of the local people I had interviewed on my show. A Czechoslovakian, Jirka had a fascinating background and profound spiritual understanding. He was also a businessman and a skilled investor. When I asked him if there was a way to invest my money to do some good, rather than putting it in a bank, Jirka's response was: "Wherever you put your money is where you put your energy. Why don't you put it into yourself?" I told him that was a good idea, but I didn't know what I wanted to do. He looked me in the eye and said, "Yes, you do. You do know what you want to do." I protested that I had been trying to figure that out for the

past couple of years. "You do know," he insisted and suggested I come back in a few days and we would talk more about it.

When I look back I see that I was like a haystack waiting for a match. When Jirka gave me permission to do what I came here to do, I went up in flames. When I walked out of his office, I did know what I wanted to do. In my mind I heard the answer: to disseminate spiritual wisdom.

But how? Three options occurred to me: books, video, or audio tapes. Books I still avoided after academia. Television I had a lot of concerns about. Audio made the most sense, partially because of my involvement with radio. I still didn't realize that my radio interview program was the beginning of the very work I was seeking to do.

I went back to Jirka two days later, clear that I would invest the money in a business to disseminate spiritual wisdom. I had only a vague idea of what that would have to do with audio tapes, however. I figured I would give the project two years, and if it didn't work out, I'd be no worse off. The money had come to me, I hadn't earned it, so I didn't really have anything to lose. He offered to rent me a small room above the health food store he was running, and Sounds True opened its doors in April, 1985. Now over a decade later, that same statement of purpose—disseminating spiritual wisdom—still guides the company.

During the first couple of years, Sounds True continued as a conference-recording service and added on a tape-duplicating business. A friend introduced me to a musician, Bill Whiteacre, who was looking for a way to duplicate and eventually record his music. We made a deal. He would work at a relatively low wage, purchasing, setting up, and maintaining all of our duplicating equipment. In exchange he could buy bulk tapes and duplicate his own music. Later, when I started traveling out of town to record seminars and workshops and needed to prepare my radio program in advance, we made another mutually beneficial deal. I would pay for the materials, and Bill would contribute the labor to build a studio where I could produce my shows and he could record his own music.

Meanwhile, I continued taping everything I could in the fields of psychology and spiritual development. I would duplicate and sell tapes to conference participants, and give copies to the lecturers with the invitation to contact me if they ever wanted to produce tapes for distribution. Many of these were the same people I eventually went back to for our first catalog. I kept master tapes of everything I did, because people would sometimes later ask for copies.

My fantasy was to expand my radio program by having a national radio show. In order to do that, we would need a catalog of programs to send out to listeners. Again, it was because of a special relationship that Sounds True took its next step. A friend introduced me to a freelance graphic artist and direct mail consultant, Devon Christensen. I showed him my archives—a wall filled with cassettes. He looked through all the names, listened to some of the tapes, and said, "You know, Tami, you are sitting on a gold mine." "I am?" I said.

"What we have to do," Devon told me, "is package these programs and distribute them through a mail order catalog." So we made an arrangement that I would edit all the tapes, and he would develop the packaging and sales copy. Thus began nine months during which I ran the company in the daytime, and at night edited tapes on a reel to reel machine, hand splicing with a razor blade. In fact, until just a few years ago when we moved to a computer system, I edited every single Sounds True tape myself.

For the next three years, Devon worked at Sounds True part-time, continuing his other work on the side to generate enough to live on. Sounds True never took out business loans but always operated off our cash flow, so I paid him a minimal amount—about $5000 for the first year, about twice as much the next two. The idea was if the catalog business became successful, Devon and I would enter into a partnership and he would own part of the company. We didn't specify what part, and we had no formal agreement. We just recognized that each of us could be trusted, and we both gave the work everything we had. It took about nine months to get the tapes edited and packaged. The first catalog came out in 1988.

By 1991, with $1.2 million in revenue, it became clear that we had a real business. It was time to change the status of the company from a sole proprietorship into a corporation. Devon asked for 20% ownership and got it, and he has remained my business partner. The thread that is woven through the entire development of Sounds True is relationship, from the help and inspiration of those who enabled and encouraged me to begin, to the trusting and willing friendships of those who have worked to build the company. The success of Sounds True is in the story of those relationships.

We're also successful because the world is hungry for the kind of spiritual information we're distributing. I know that Sounds True has a very bright future because this is God's work we're doing, bringing beautiful and inspiring information to people. Clearly, this is what I am supposed to do. I can't imagine doing anything else.

JENAI LANE

Respect
San Francisco, California

"Respect knows no color, creed, race, gender . . ." So reads the calling card

for Jenai Lane's company which creates affordable jewelry with a message:

respect for ourselves and the environment. Her designs, packaged with back-

ground information, feature symbols from across time and cultures. Jenai

has a background in documentary film and produced the award-winning

Don't Be a T.V.: Television Victim *and* Warning: the Media May

be Hazardous to Your Health. *Starting with $3000 in capital, Respect*

grew to more than $1 million in sales in two years, and was selected in 1995

by Entrepreneur magazine as one of the 50 Fastest-Growing Small

Businesses in America. Jenai has been named a 1997 Entrepeneur of the

Year by the National Association of Women Business Owners.

As a documentary filmmaker, my passion has been to raise awareness and get out a message, and I look at Respect as a way to do that. It's not just a business to make jewelry or a profit. For example, I've created an Endangered Species line that's packaged with information on how to get involved, with 10% of profits donated to the cause. We did a Mother's Day pin, called the Great Mother, with profits going to the Family Violence Prevention Fund. We also give money off the top of our sales to non-profits. This past year I got to write checks for substantial amounts of money to over ten different organizations—that's my favorite thing to do. But five years ago when I was studying Marxism in college, if you had told me I'd be a full-fledged capitalist selling a product, I would never have believed it, never. I have seen, however, that I can be socially responsible and still make money. I produce a product that doesn't pollute the environment, we treat our employees really well, we educate the public and we give out money to nonprofits. So it's advantageous for everyone in the long run.

Working as a woman in the film industry convinced me that I wanted to be my own boss. In Hollywood, I could see that the kinds of films I wanted to make weren't going to be financed there.

So I got a job with a film company in San Francisco in feature film development and video distribution and did some freelance video production on the side. One morning before work when I was taking a shower, my eye fell on the little chain connected to the bathtub stopper. I put it around my neck with the stopper hanging off. "Wow, this could be a fantastic necklace," I thought. It was so industrial and kind of hip.

I had never been involved in jewelry making, but just for fun, I went to the hardware store and got ball chain in different sizes and shapes, and "O" rings and various metal objects, and put them together to wear. When my friends liked what I'd done, I thought maybe I had something going. Not much was happening at work—my boss was out a lot, and I'd get everything done and have nothing to do. So I used the extra time to design a line of jewelry which I took to small boutiques and crafts fairs. Early on, I saw that the jewelry could have social impact, and I designed a product to promote AIDS awareness and raise money for people with AIDS.

I was getting such a positive response to my jewelry that I thought, "Wow, I have a hot product. If I can get this off the ground, I can finance my filmmaking in the future." I knew nothing about business. My degree was in socio/political media. But I love a good challenge. I started reading books and talking to people. I had a $3000 settlement from a car accident, and I decided to use that to buy supplies. I had to buy all pre-made designs because I couldn't afford to have molds custom-made for my own designs.

I enlisted my friends to come over and assemble jewelry in the living room of my one-bedroom apartment. The place was hysterical. Ball chain and jump rings were all over the place. My bedroom was the editing studio for my video productions, and there was nowhere to get away from it all.

About six months into this, I began wondering how I could expand my customer base. I thought it would be a good idea to approach the major department stores, but I didn't know how. I was sitting in a cafe, thinking about what my next move should be, when I saw a woman walking down the street with jewelry hanging off a big rack. It looked like my kind of stuff, with ball chain and other similar things. I jumped up and went after her. "What are you doing with the jewelry?" I asked, when I stopped her. She said, "I'm a sales rep. I sell it to department stores." That was such a synchronistic event that obviously it was meant to be. Jane Barry took on my line and immediately brought it to the big players. In fact, she was such a good sales person that I couldn't afford to pay her a commission, so I made her a partner in the company.

I needed some real capital to buy supplies in order to continue meeting sales demands. I took my business plan and my sales records and went to the bank I had been associated with for six years. They laughed me out the door. "You don't have any collateral, you're too young, you have no experience." I felt really angry. I was asking for a small amount of money—$10,000—and I could demonstrate my sales and the demand for the product. Just because I was a young woman without a lot of experience didn't mean I was a bad risk. I went to three banks before I gave that avenue up.

I'm the kind of person who looks at an obstacle as something to get around. I was raised by a single parent and am the oldest child. We didn't have a lot of money, and I learned early on to be self-sufficient and not expect ever to be dependent upon a man or anyone else. Growing up in a survival mode, I learned how to make things work. I learned that even if everyone says no, no, no, *you* know that there's got to be a yes somewhere or somehow. There had to be some kind of support for small businesses. I looked in the telephone book and found several programs. I checked them all out, and one of them, a nonprofit called Women's Initiative for Self Employment (WISE) seemed the best.

They did give loans but required taking two courses they offered in business planning to become eligible. I worked very hard in those courses to flesh out my business plan and make it really good. At the end, I had to go before the board and present my product and the plan. It was a great moment when I found out that I would receive the loan. Finally someone believed in me.

With that first loan of $2000, I bought supplies, and I paid WISE back in 90 days. I was still making things at home. With each order I would take out a loan to buy supplies, then pay off the loan with sales. My second loan from WISE jumped up to $10,000 and I hired other companies to do the casting of my designs and the manufacturing of the jewelry. It was great to get it out of my living room.

Moving to the next level, however, I learned a very hard lesson. Basically not having done anything like this before, I had to do tons of research to find out how to go about it. But I hadn't found out that I needed a non-disclosure agreement when I took my designs to a caster, and my designs and ideas were ripped off by someone who started their own line with them.

I've learned a lot of things the hard way. I started out wanting to be egalitarian as a boss, and learned that it didn't work. Some kind of structure and definition, although not necessarily hierarchical, was necessary to make things run smoothly and efficiently. But I know that all the skills I am learning in business, I can apply to producing films in the future. And I'm certainly coming up with good material for future films—I'm still asked at tradeshows if I am the salesgirl. I guess people don't expect a young woman to be the president of a company.

It's really important to me that my product serves a bigger purpose. The world doesn't need another tzotchke, but if we can use the jewelry as a vehicle for change, that makes it worthwhile. My feeling is that people want jewelry that means something to them. So I've done a lot of research to bring in symbols from cultures and religions around the world. I think it's a way of bringing global spirituality to the mainstream. We have so much to learn from other cultures, and I've always been interested in diversity. In fact, with my skin coloring, I could be from a lot of different ethnic backgrounds. The most asked question of my life has been: "What are you?" I am a Russian-Hungarian Jew, but people often think I'm Hispanic and speak to me in Spanish. When I traveled in Turkey, everyone thought I was Turkish; in Italy I was Italian.

The thumbprint that is Respect's logo came out of a similar vein. Everyone has a thumb print, and when you look at it, you can't tell if it's from the hand of someone black or white, man or woman, straight or gay, rich or poor. Yet each is unique.

I've always considered respect for others as basic. When I was living in London in the Black community, people would greet me and each other by saying, "Respect." I thought that was the coolest thing I had ever heard. It was like reminding people everyday that we all deserve respect. I thought, "If I ever have a company, that's exactly what I'm going to call it."

Although the fundamental principles of Respect never change, I've begun applying the Respect trademark of forward-looking products to other markets, specifically, the computer accessory market. The idea for the Respect® LapPak came about out of personal need. I looked everywhere for a bag that I could carry my laptop in, and there was nothing on the market that didn't hurt my back or didn't make me look like an accountant, so I designed one.

We have added fashion into a product category that has been traditionally devoid of style and fun. I love this bag!

I've always seen myself working for myself. I wanted to create my own environment and do it my own way. I'm setting goals for myself so that I don't lose sight of my dream of starting a film production company. My jewelry company is making a difference, and I know I can make a huge impact with the films I want to do.

NABILA MANGO

Mango Trading Services
San Francisco, California

Mango Trading Services evolved from a distributor of Arabic books during the '80s into a exporter of computer products to Arabic countries. Nabila Mango has kept her business deliberately small, acquiring her clients through personal contacts and working with part-time employees out of her home office. Working from home enabled her to be present when her young daughter, who is now at boarding school, returned each day from school.

I became a businesswoman through necessity. My undergraduate and graduate training was in library science and Middle Eastern languages and literature which would have prepared me for work in an academic library. When I was newly married, I moved with my husband to the Bay Area, hoping to avoid the kind of prejudice I had faced in the Midwest, as an Arab, a Palestinian, and a Muslim. Two local university positions were open for Arabic and Middle Eastern Collections, and I applied, hopeful because they exactly suited my skills and experience. In both cases, men were chosen over all other qualified female librarians. In one instance the job went to a man who in fact had to return to library school to obtain a key qualification he was missing. Those avenues closed to me, I had to look around for another way of earning a living. I realized that as an entrepreneur, I would be less vulnerable to the kind of discrimination I had encountered in academic settings.

For a librarian, what commodity would seem more natural than books? So I investigated the potential of importing Arabic books from the Middle East. As a young adult in Jordan, my interest in books and reading had attracted the attention of the staff in the college I was attending. I had been planning to become a pharmacist, but some Americans on staff suggested I apply to schools in the United States for a scholarship to study library science. I did, and received a scholarship to a college in New Jersey. My family's first reaction was that I was too young to go alone to the United States, but they agreed in the end, thinking it would be for only one year.

Education was very important to my family, as it was to other Palestinian families who had lost their homes in the Arab-Israeli war. When I was growing up, my parents would tell us, my four sisters and my brother, "We don't know where you are going to end up, but if you are educated, no matter where you are, whether you are in America or Australia or wherever, you will be able to stand on your own feet." We were so young, we didn't even know what America or Australia was, but we learned that education was important. So while it was not typical for a Palestinian family at that time to educate five girls in the way we were educated, it was typical for them to have the education of their children as their main goal in life.

I stayed on to complete my bachelor's degree in library science, graduating in June of 1967, just in time for another Arab-Israeli war. My parents telephoned me not to come home. Their business had suffered heavily, with large stocks warehoused in the West Bank lost to them. The influx of thousands of refugees had destabilized the country. I should stay in America, they said, and continue on to graduate school. That summer, however, working at a university library in Philadelphia was a baptism by fire. Feelings ran high on both sides after the June war, and I received harassment and telephone threats that required me to recruit male students on campus to ride home with me on the bus at night after work.

So for me, many years later, starting my own business had the promise of being able to avoid the humiliation I had experienced through discrimination. The move from academe to commerce was a natural one for me. My family on both sides had been merchants in Jaffa for many generations. I had friends and relatives throughout the Middle East, so I established the connections I needed to begin importing books from the Arab world and selling them to colleges and universities, to researchers, and throughout the Arab-American community in the United States and Canada. I traveled to conferences all over North America to display and sell books and, between conferences, sold them by mail order. This was very satisfying to my love of books, but not very lucrative. It was hard to charge what it cost to cover shipping costs, particularly because the quality of the books, in terms of paper and printing, was beneath American standards. I began to lose money and even though my heart was in it, I knew I would need to change my business.

When I found that children's and women's clothing from America had a market in the Arab world, I began exporting that. Then, as Middle Eastern friends started returning home to do business after getting their Ph.D.s in American universities, they took their personal computers with them, thereby creating a new need I could fill. Because we lived in Silicon Valley, these friends began calling me, asking if I could find them certain memory boards. I had discovered my real niche. Whenever I traveled to the Arab world, I expanded my contacts until the export and resale of computer hardware and software became a viable business enterprise. I concentrated mainly on the Arab countries because I could speak the language, I understood the culture, and I knew what it takes to establish the trust on which to base a business deal. When my husband lost his own business, he worked with me for a couple of years until we divorced.

My business then became a real necessity as I supported my daughter as well as myself. It was one of the biggest challenges of my life to run a business in a field in which I had had no training whatsoever. I had never taken a computer course, and I needed to teach myself everything. However, I enjoy challenges, and this one has given meaning to my pursuit and great satisfaction as I have succeeded in it. I have learned the product, I have learned the market, and I know where to buy and how to sell. I have also learned how to cope with the attitude that is most often apparent in this male-dominated business—of underestimating the intelligence and capability of women simply because of their gender.

There have been other unforeseen challenges. Reminiscent of my father's business losses during Arab-Israeli conflicts, I suffered considerable losses at the time of the Gulf War. I had just shipped off a major consignment of goods to Kuwait the day before Saddam Hussein's army marched in. It was many months before I saw any portion of the money I had laid out.

I kept my office in my home so that I could be there when my daughter returned from school. That meant that the business remained relatively small. That is a disadvantage on one hand, because it has necessitated my wearing other hats as well—acting as a consultant to help people develop marketing plans and teaching Arabic at San Francisco State University. But I am a natural teacher, and I am never completely happy if teaching is not some part of my regular activities. On the other hand, the advantage of having a small clientele is that the business is not consuming enough to keep me from the work that gives real meaning to my life—active involvement in Arab-American academic, cultural and human rights organizations.

While I have not become the professor and bibliographer I was trained to be, I feel very fortunate that I have been able to succeed and stand on my feet by having my own business, and I want other women, especially Arab American women, to know that they too can do this through their own ingenuity and determination. My mission is to be a good role model for young Arab-American and Muslim women, and thus my next goal has become to train as a therapist and counselor and move beyond my export business to work with young women. My soul has suffered by having a finger pointed at me as personally responsible anytime something happens in the Middle East. I wonder at those times, "Where do I belong? Where can I go?" This country is now my home. So I constantly strive to feel stronger emotionally about my own identity, and it gives my life meaning to reach out to young people who might experience the same questions. Working for myself has given me the freedom to do this.

PATRICE WYNNE

GAIA Bookstore and Community Center
Berkeley, California

More than a purveyor of books and resources, GAIA is the hub of a spiritual/

social/ecological community. Opened in 1987, it is one of the nation's leading

independently owned bookstores in the field of contemporary spirituality and

alternative lifestyles. GAIA's shelves hold more than 14,000 titles on health,

spirituality, business, psychology, world religions, community, culture, and

politics. Company values, personnel practices, store events, and local and

global service activities arise from Patrice's passionate commitment to

building community.

I didn't study how to do a business. It came to me in the process of living my life. When I was two years old, my family moved to Levittown, Pennsylvania, leaving behind Minersville, a beautiful little town built into a hillside. My grandmother lived in one of the town's small houses, close enough for neighbors to have conversations with each other from their porches and across their fences. Each time I went back to visit her, I could feel the profound sense of *belonging* in Minersville. It had the seeds and roots of community. In Levittown, on the other hand, all the houses were identical, and the sense of isolation was pervasive. One of my earliest memories is looking out of our very large picture window and seeing in the leveled fields a vast expanse of emptiness. In leaving Minersville I had lost something that connected me to the earth and to life. Many years later, GAIA Bookstore, named after the ancient Greek goddess of the Earth, would become for me not just a business but an expression of the sense of community and connection with nature that I carry with me from my earliest days.

I certainly didn't plan to have a bookstore with a community focus. I simply made a series of choices in my life based on what I felt passionate about. Often that meant groping through a lot of unknowns. Only in retrospect do I see a pattern and direction in those choices. Instead of going to college immediately after high school, I took a job with Fotomat, a company that was operating a national chain of kiosks to provide photographic film and processing. After a couple of years there, they offered me a position as a supervisor in the San Francisco Bay Area. It was my ticket out of Levittown. By the time I was thirty, I owned my own home, drove a BMW—and had spent more than a decade focused entirely on my job. I had no friends outside the company. All my relationships with men were shaped by how well they fit into my work schedule. In essence, since arriving in California, I hadn't lived much beyond the 50 miles my job encompassed. At my core lived a very empty and lonely person.

The wake-up call was sharp and real and painful. It was excruciating to realize that I had no bonds connecting me to anything I really cared about. Each day I got up and performed the duties and activities I was responsible for, but there was no deep, caring, loving community in my life. Who was this person I had become? To what end was this pursuit? It wasn't that my job had robbed my soul; I had willingly turned my soul over by not developing other aspects of myself. Resigning from my position was dramatic and frightening, because I didn't have anything else to go toward. I just knew I had to let go of that boulder that was holding me in a place that wasn't my own.

After a couple semesters of college, I dropped out and left for Europe. I needed time for reflection, to be without an agenda, to let the spirit move me, to see what emerged when I wasn't embedded in this culture and its values. When I returned after six months, I gravitated toward the spiritual feminist community in the Bay Area—students, writers, teachers who were on fire with their vision. A whole new world began opening up to me—the female spirit and symbols, goddess and earth-based religions, new ways of praying, new perspectives on history. I enrolled again in college, designing my own major in women's studies with an emphasis on women's spirituality. I became involved in political and social action. I had no idea where I was going. I was simply following what felt right and honorable, passionate and exciting.

That led me after graduation to a rural retreat and conference center where I was asked to create a bookstore. Within one year I had established a thriving business. It became clear to me that I had a passion for and commitment to the spiritual journey as well as knowledge and talents in the business world. Now I needed to put them together. A friend offered me a place to live on his beautiful land in Northern California, and I decided to start my own mail order business, offering books and other items connected with women's spirituality. I would call it "Awaken Goddess Wisdom."

I didn't know a thing about running a catalog company, but I believe that there are talents that function like instincts. Paul Hawken, author of *Growing a Business,* calls them "trade skills." When my father was laid off after years of working for the steel industry, he directed his outrage and disappointment into starting his own business. Growing up around him shaped the way I have moved in my own work. I trust my work skills, I trust my networking and research skills. I trust that things come to me that I don't ask for consciously. And I trust that when I choose a path, I can follow it into the unknown.

The path of starting a mail order business took a completely unexpected turn. I had borrowed a pick-up truck to get my first mail order catalog from the printers. On the way back home the brakes went out and the truck plunged 200 feet over a cliff above the Pacific Ocean. When you are in a vehicle that's flying over the edge of a cliff, any delusions you might have about being in control

171

of your actions or your life are gone. My body was screaming in terror, "Surrender, surrender, let go!" but I was passionately holding onto life.

The truck landed upright between two trees that were sticking out of the cliffside. It felt to me as if those trees had grasped the sides of the truck and said, "We've got you in our arms. You're not going any farther. We *want* you." When the vehicle stopped, I was in complete delirium. I understood, in every part of my being, what a gift it is to be given life. Ecstatic and sobbing, I climbed out the back window of the cab, climbed up the grassy cliffside, scattered with copies of my mail order brochure, and hitched a ride home.

At that point my life turned around. I knew I had Work here to do. It was like being told "Enough of ditzing around. You have been given a life. Make your contribution."

Not long after, I was asked by a major publisher who had seen my catalog to write a guide to the tools and resources for the burgeoning women's spirituality movement. Without hesitation, even though I had no idea how to write such a book, I said yes. I moved to Berkeley to begin. My mail order products now filled every nook and cranny in my house in Berkeley. I left the front door unlocked so local people could come in to buy things directly off the shelves. A note on the door asked them to leave the money for their purchases on the couch. Meanwhile I was in the back room, working on my book.

Three years later, *The WomanSpirit Sourcebook* was published, a compendium of the books and organizations and people and music of the women's spirituality movement. In writing it, I had come to understand the whole network that comprised the new feminist and earth-centered spirituality. By the time the book was published I had met Eric Joost, who would later become my husband, and with his encouragement decided to gather all the resources of that movement together and put them into an environment called GAIA Bookstore. I wanted to go beyond feminist spirituality, bringing in spiritual traditions from a multitude of cultures. I wanted men to feel as comfortable as women in the store, I wanted it to be a resource and center for families, for elders, for anyone who sought sustenance within a spiritual framework.

One day after we'd been hunting for some time for the right location, Eric and I saw a "For lease" sign on an empty store front in our own neighborhood. I wrote immediately to the owner. It turned out that his sister was a Roman Catholic nun who was familiar with my mail order catalog. She convinced him he should give us the space. I was barely able to scrape together the first month's rent—all my energy had gone into the book, and my catalog orders had slowed to a crawl. Eric designed the interior and built all the shelves in our garage during time off his regular job. Over the years I had developed a great mailing list, and I sent out a large mailing announcing the opening of GAIA. The bookstore was successful from the start. A year later, Eric joined me as business partner. We've been working side by side ever since.

Aware of the core of suffering that came from being raised in an isolating suburban atmosphere, I feel passionate about building a business rooted in a community of the sacred. The store has expanded not only into a bigger location and broader inventory, but it has also become a community center, a base for events, gatherings, ceremonies, and service activities.

When I look back, I see that it's almost as if the template for GAIA Bookstore was there all along, waiting to come into existence. It was there when I was two years old looking sadly at the leveled fields and rows of identical houses in Levittown. It was there at 17 when I delighted in running my tiny Fotomat kiosk. The seed for GAIA was in the bookstore I was asked to create at the conference center. My mail order catalog and then my book carried that seed along.

One of my basic understandings about starting a business is that it's creating itself long before you open your doors. You're doing it when you've made connections or networked or had conversations across the dinner table about your dreams and ideas. You're doing it by the questions, explorations, readings, stories—all the things you do as a human being to expand your awareness of something outside yourself. You may not know that you know your business until you make the decision to start it. But once you commit yourself, you realize how many choices have been made all along to bring it into reality.

RAYDEAN ACEVEDO

Research Management Consultants, Inc. (RMCI)
Golden, Colorado

RMCI, with more than 300 employees in offices around the nation, works with clients in both the public and the private sector to minimize and clean up environmental hazards as well as to install and maintain communications systems. Among her numerous awards, Raydean Acevedo was recognized as the SBA's Los Angeles District Minority Small Business Person of the Year in 1990. The many boards she serves on include the National Women's Business Council, the National Advisory Council of the SBA, and the Hispanic Association of Colleges and Universities.

From the time I was very young, my parents said to me, "You were put on this planet to make a difference. We don't care what path you choose, but you must make the world a better place." Every day, in everything I do, I think about that—how I interact with my staff, how I interact with my clients, how all of us perform. My parents, both school teachers, were exceptional role models. I watched these two compassionate, caring individuals live a life of service. That model of achievement and dedication to serving others has given me my own very strong sense of serving. This is what led me to start my own company in order to provide a level of service that surpasses expectations, and does so in a way that benefits everyone involved, clients and employees alike.

After receiving a Masters degree and completing all but the dissertation on my Doctorate in the social sciences, I worked in that field for a number of years, doing training, technical assistance, research and analysis. I liked the work and consistently received promotions and financial rewards. One day the head of the research division I was in invited me to direct sales and marketing in a new organization he was forming in the field of advanced data processing. Even though this would mean a move out of the social sciences, I was aware that data processing would be a tremendous area of growth in the future. The new position would also mean working more directly with people. Doing research, I might not see the results of my efforts for five, even ten years down the road. I wanted more immediate and tangible feedback. I took the position.

I had no sales and marketing training and absolutely no business background. My new employer said, "I have no time to train you. You're going to have to hit the ground running." I immediately enrolled in a data processing course at the local community college to learn the vocabulary and the issues I would be dealing with. At work, if I didn't know an answer for a client, I would find it out and call them back. Or if I didn't have what they needed, I would find someone who did. My job was to serve people's needs, and I worked very hard at it. Customers would say, "No one has ever given us this kind of service. You are always there, early morning, late at night, weekends." And I loved it. To me, providing high quality service was fulfilling the purpose my parents had talked about.

I continued to grow in my responsibilities and receive promotions, but something was missing. My philosophy is that business is about helping people become successful. Success, in my mind, is defined as empowerment, individual development, and opportunity to contribute—and that goes for employees, clients and the greater community. I have always believed in helping all those with whom I interact to reach beyond themselves. But I didn't see opportunities to do that in the environment in which I was working. I was a top performer myself, but I didn't see the chance for that experience being extended to or encouraged in others. I didn't want to just talk about quality management, teamwork, and excellence, I wanted to implement them. I decided to form my own company in order to make that happen.

When the president got wind of my plans to leave, he called me and said, "Please don't leave. How much money will it take? Tell me your price." I said to him, "I'm not running away from you. I am going to build something that I have always wanted to build. I thank you very much for your support, but this is what I am doing."

In 1987 I started my own company. In the beginning, our product was software systems and training. But I think you have to be constantly looking ahead to see what opportunities are coming up and then be very willing to take risks. I read constantly, talked with and listened to people, basically doing continual market analysis. You might have a great product, but if you don't understand the market, nobody knows about it, or you might provide great service, but if nobody wants your product, it won't sell. So I was constantly asking what do people need? What kinds of services are needed and who is providing them? Can we make a contribution here? What I saw coming up on the horizon was the need for environmental services and telecommunications.

I have always been concerned about environments and our ability to impact them, whether that means interacting with people in the context of the workplace or the effect of a highly industrialized nation on natural resources and the planet we occupy. I wanted to surround myself with highly qualified technical people who can provide the kinds of services that are required in a rapidly changing world, people with the ability to make a difference in that arena.

I began to identify the leaders in the industry and those with good reputations, those who were committed to their clients and their services and those with technical expertise. I showed them the foundation we had to support them and created a team that together could be successful. We work with our clients in everything from environmental planning, regulatory compliance and pollution prevention to asbestos services, hazardous waste engineering, and lead-based paint abatement. We perform these services across the nation and also in other parts of the world. Our excellence in logistics management means that we are called upon in fires, floods, hurricanes, and other crises. We know how to get people where they need to go. After a major California earthquake, we had people on-site within hours, analyzing the situation, stabilizing the sites, and supervising the clean-up. Our telecommunications division functions as a separate entity, creating high technology telephone communications networks, installing, maintaining, and operating the services.

RMCI is very successful, despite the many challenges for women in business. There is of course the fact that we still are not recognized by men for our capabilities. I was at a meeting in the aerospace industry a couple of years ago. The gentleman next to me asked me who I worked for. I told him RMCI, and in response to his questions went on and told him what the company does. He said, "It sounds like a pretty impressive company." I said, "It is." "Well, do you have a business card?" he asked. I handed him my card. He looked at the card, he looked over at me, he looked back down at the card again with a very perplexed look on his face. My card, of course, indicated that I was CEO/President of the company. "Is this your card?" he asked.

As a woman in business, I realize I have to be the best I can be, because I am representing many, many others. Whether I want to be or not, I am regarded as a model of women in business. In my case, I have the opportunity to be a model for what is best about minority women, in particular Hispanic women. To me that's a very special opportunity, and I take that responsibility very seriously.

I work twelve to fourteen hours a day, Monday through Friday; on Saturdays and Sundays, I work from four to ten hours each day. What keeps me going is the belief that we are providing a very special environment in which to work and extremely high quality service to our customers. We are making a difference.

MARJORIE KELLY

Business Ethics Magazine
Minneapolis, Minnesota

From a spare bedroom in her home in 1987, Marjorie Kelly launched a newsletter that would become Business Ethics, *the first national magazine especially for people involved in socially responsible business and investment. As concern for the environment and humane values has continued to move into mainstream business practices, Ms. Kelly has laid plans to rename her magazine* Good Business, *and reposition it to serve people throughout the business world who are interested in integrating positive values into their work. Among other service involvements, she serves on the board of the National Institute for a New Corporate Vision.*

reached a point in my mid 30s when I started seriously asking myself, "What's worth doing with my life?" I carried that question around for a couple of years, trying out different answers to see if they fit. I kept deepening the question: What is it I really want? Not what I once wanted, or am supposed to want, or what other people think I should want. But what do I really want? I realized I was not going to get very many chances in my life to answer that question, because if I started something at all significant, it would probably take me ten years to pull it off. At that age, how many ten-year paths would I have?

It became clear to me that at the most basic level, what I wanted to do was make as big a difference as I possibly could. Archimedes said that if he had a lever long enough he could single-handedly move the world. It wasn't that I single-handedly wanted to move the world, but I sensed that the world was moving, something was beginning to shift, and I wanted to help clarify that shift and move it along. But how? What was my lever? It turned out to be business.

The one thing I did know at the time, and had always known, was that I wanted to be in publishing. I have a Masters Degree in Journalism, and I love publishing. After graduation I worked at several newspapers, then got a job at a company in Madison, Wisconsin, that created newsletters for higher education and for business. My goal at the time was to work part-time and do free-lance writing on the side, so I took a job as a secretary, not telling my boss I had a Masters. When I came up with a good idea for a newsletter for educators, however, my true colors emerged, and he promoted me to the full-time position of Associate Publisher, in charge of new projects. My job was to look for emerging trends and create newsletters in response. In order to do that I got on every possible mailing list and scanned the tons of newsletters and magazines I received.

That was during the early to mid-'80s. I noticed increasing talk about empowering employees, social investing, feminine style management, South African divestment, and all the rest. Socially responsible business was on the rise, and businesses were starting to have ethics programs. All of this seemed different from the classic style of business I had previously been reading about. I could see the door opening for a new way of perceiving business, and I wanted my work to help open that door. In that realization the personal and the professional came together for me. I saw something that looked worth doing, and I saw a niche in need of an information product.

My boss, however, didn't get it. If I was going to do this project, I knew I would have to do it on my own. I come from a long line of entrepreneurs, and I had always thought it would be nice to have my own business. So I cut my hours back to part-time and set out to start what would eventually become *Business Ethics* magazine. I wanted a forum where business people could talk together about managing in new ways. Instead of throwing stones at the citadel of power—as so many activists did—I wanted to stand inside the halls of power and explore with other business people how we make these changes.

My family lent me $15,000, a bank gave me a $5000 loan, and I set up an office in the spare bedroom of my house. Since I'd been creating professional newsletters for years, my initial concept was to publish a 16-page newsletter, with no advertising, and charge a typical business newsletter price of $97 a year. I rented some target mailing lists, and received a 5% response to my direct mail campaign, which in the business is extremely good. I was off to a decent beginning.

My tendency is to be a loner, so at first the publication was really a one-person operation. I had to learn how to ask for help and to accept it. A friend of mine, Miriam, started coming by to help out. I remember the first time I overheard her explaining to someone on the phone what *Business Ethics* was, I was amazed that she got it right. I had thought I was the only one who knew how to do that. Miriam eventually became my partner, and I know I couldn't have done it without her. We're genuinely co-founders.

And it was pretty grueling. There is a very high failure rate in magazines. They look like a lot of fun to do, but they are labor and capital intensive, very hard to pull off. And I was facing a double risk. Not only was I starting a new company, subject to all the vicissitudes any young business encounters, but I was also trying to carve out a niche for a whole new way of thinking about business. Because I had chosen so carefully what I wanted, my depth of commitment pulled me through the hard times. But I would read wonderful stories about people whose businesses were soaring and think, "What's wrong with me?" When we get into these very tough situations, it's easy to think "I'm the only one screwing up." It's important for entrepreneurs to tell each other that it can be so hard—and that if we are doing something we are deeply committed to and stick with it, we'll succeed. Most business owners who fail simply give up too soon.

After a year and a half, I ran out of money. I had been getting a tremendous response from my readers, corporate executives from businesses large and small—many at Fortune 500 firms. They would call up and say, "I can hardly believe a magazine like this exists. I don't feel alone anymore." And they would send in notes with their renewal checks saying, "I've got to have this magazine, but why is it so darn expensive?" So I knew I was doing something right—and I knew I was doing something wrong.

I decided to stop publishing for a month or two, get advice from people in the publishing business, and try to raise some money. The month turned into a year as I traveled all over the country, running up my credit cards, talking to anybody in the publishing business who was willing to give me advice. Miriam meanwhile took a job at a meat-packing plant to pay for the mortgage on the house where we now both lived and where the business was set up. Every month I scraped together enough through consulting jobs to pay off my printer and other suppliers.

We were seriously broke. I remember Miriam and I cashing in pop bottles so we could eat at McDonald's. I had already borrowed too much money from my family. Of course, I could have gone out and gotten a job, but I *needed* to do this magazine. I didn't know how I was going to do it, but I was intent on it, and I was not going to stop.

Finally, a man in California said, "I really like what you're doing and want to support it, but I don't want to invest in it. If I do, then I have to track the investment and worry about whether or not I'm going to get a return for my money. I'd rather just give you

$10,000, and my only stipulation is that you match it." I went to the Twin Cities in neighboring Minnesota and found a business incubator—a building set up with support services for entrepreneurs—run by a private college, the University of St. Thomas. They decided to match the grant with in-kind services, such as rent and the use of facilities. That meant moving to Minneapolis, which we welcomed. On Christmas Day, I was showing my house to renters, and by New Year's Day, we were gone.

It turned out that the move was fortuitous. There is an older generation of businessmen in the Twin Cities who are very committed to humane values. Many of my investors have been part of that group—retired CEOs who went out of their way to support a woman-run company and new values in business.

With enough money for one issue, we started up again, with a new format, double the number of pages and half the price. Once the issue was out, we sat down to figure out what was needed for a direct mailing to build our subscriber base. It would cost $14,500, and we didn't know where we were going to get it. Later that same week I got a call from my brother Matt, saying, "Have you checked your mail yet? We've just inherited some money from Grandpa." My grandfather had left preferred stock for his fifteen grandchildren and it had come to maturity just at that point. Each of us had inherited $14,500. Miriam and I looked at each other and just rolled on the floor laughing.

There has always been this kind of miraculous feeling about *Business Ethics*. When we really needed something, it came through. I believe that if I am doing something that in my deepest self I know I need to do, then that's the thing that the world needs me to do too, and the world will assist me.

CAROL RIVENDELL
& MARTHA LINDT

Wild Women Adventures
Sebastopol, California

Carol Rivendell and Martha Lindt have combined their respective skills as

psychotherapist and travel agent to create a tour company for women that

enjoins the traveler to "explore the world and find yourself"—while having

fun. Zany fun. In addition to being a full-service travel agency, Wild

Women Adventures offers "Insanity with Dignity" Tours for groups of 6–10

women to places both on- and off-the-beaten-track. From Mexico to Europe

to Tibet, these unique tours provide a hassle-free opportunity to "exhilarate

your spirit, dazzle your senses and pacify your mind."

Martha and I met when our teenage children were dating. Our phone conversations about our kids turned into the friendship and business partnership that sprouted Wild Women Adventures. For seven years Martha had been operating a successful full-service travel agency, and for the previous twenty, I had been working as a psychotherapist and conducting personal growth seminars. Both of us were ready for a change. Martha had gone into the travel business because she likes to travel (and her husband doesn't), but sitting in a chair all day selling tickets was not what she'd had in mind when she started. For me, the death of a dear friend was the jolt that started a new direction in my life. My first thought after Michael died was, "Thank God he was such an *alive* person." As I walked out of the hospital that day, I made a promise to myself: "I'm not going to waste any more time on crap." Both Martha and I had been asking ourselves, "What are we doing—waiting for things to look easy before we do what we want to with our lives? Our simultaneous answer was, "No, we're going to do it *now*."

When I suggested one afternoon that it would be more fun and relaxing—for everyone, including me—to do a seminar for women in some gorgeous place in Hawaii, Martha jumped on the idea.

"Let's do it. And why limit the seminars to Hawaii? Why not do them all over the world?" By the end of that same afternoon, we had the itinerary for our first Kauai seminar and tickets for our first mission to Europe to scout out other locations. We just stepped off the curb and went for it, and that's how we've worked together ever since. When we get an idea, we just do it.

That was March, 1994. A little over a month later, on May 1, we got our fictitious business name. Martha had been reading a book entitled *A Whistling Woman Is Up To No Good: Finding Your Wild Woman.* In it the author, Laurel King, wrote: "A wild woman is extraordinarily herself. She does what is natural to her without inhibitions, which means she can do and be anything." We thought "That's what we're going to do—take women in search of their natural healthy selves." We needed to convey the right image for that in our advertising—something that suggested breaking out of our habits and ruts—so we bought silly hats and blouses and had passport pictures taken to make a quick brochure. Our first Wild Woman Tour was on its way.

By the time we got back from our fact-finding tour to Paris and Greece, our idea had evolved from seminars for women held in various locations to "Why don't we just take women to great places and have fun?" What could be better than travel for personal growth, self-esteem, and nurturing? Women are so used to taking care of others. Just the act of doing something so spectacular for themselves as traveling to some fantastic place is a way of saying, "I'm worth it. Life is filled with joy and I'm going to go get some."

That's when Carmen Miranda became our inspiration. She was a dancer, singer, comedienne and actress—obviously a wild woman. At times I've said to clients in therapy, "Now what would Carmen Miranda, or Katherine Hepburn, or Lucille Ball do in a situation like the one you're in?" Taking on a persona, adopting an attitude, can do a lot to shift a person's perspective. So the "Carmen Miranda" photo of Martha and me became our Wild Women trademark. However, the professional brochure company we went to for help with our first real brochure didn't quite see our point. To them, a professional image had to be serious and corporate-looking. We decided that instead of paying them the $3000 they wanted to produce a brochure, we'd take our chances, do it on our own, and with the money saved, send it out to more people.

We set up an office in a room off my garage, and Martha divided her time between her travel agency and our burgeoning tour company. When Martha got notice that the rent was going up on the office of her travel agency, she felt as if life had tossed her a lemon. I made the lemonade and suggested we open one office for both businesses. Again, we didn't spend time talking about it. We just went right out to look at a place for rent in the center of town. It had a purple carpet, which was perfect. We spent half an hour designing areas for bookshelves, cabinets, a couch and table, and we had our new office. That's our style. If it feels right, we just do it. We can't afford to be afraid to make a mistake.

The only thing we do seem to be serious about is money. We've spent all our own money on getting our tour company going. I've used my income and savings, Martha has used her income and credit cards. In our second year, we got a line of credit from our friendly neighborhood bank. Martha's husband, who has a very successful business, points out that it is important to keep worry and negativity out of the picture. So we don't dwell on the fact that many small businesses fail. We figure that if the company doesn't become what we think it's going to be, something else valuable will happen in its place. We've found that we bolster each other through

the hard times, and we know that if we weren't doing this together, there would be no hope of doing it at all. So we also plan on succeeding together. Neither one of us wants to end up as an old woman eating cat food—despite the fact that, as Martha points out, there are some very good cat foods out there.

Our first year in business, we made a commitment to ourselves that if we offered a trip and only one person signed up for it, we would go. And that's exactly what did happen. Our first "Erin Go Braghless" tour to Ireland cost us a lot of money, but we had a great time with our one adventurous wild woman traveler. Right from the beginning, we've stayed very clear about our goals, which are to be dependable and professional in everything we do, and to know that on every trip we take, we learn something no matter what happens—so we keep a sense of humor in the process.

As part of product development we scout out each place where we're planning a tour—to locate unique accommodations, the best places to eat, the least touristy attractions if possible, and the best pastry shops. On one of our first fact-finding missions, we had been staying in a wonderful little castle in the Loire Valley in France. We were on the train back to Paris to catch our 3:30 p.m. flight to Ireland. One hour into the trip, I realized I had forgotten my purse with passport and a thousand dollars back at the castle. Not only would we have to return, we would likely miss our flight, losing valuable scouting time in Ireland. I was horrified, thinking I had ruined everything. Martha's immediate response was, "Great! We don't know what's going to happen the rest of the day!" The worst-case scenario, she pointed out, would be having to spend the night in Paris. Now was that a hardship? So instead of me continuing to beat myself up, we worked out a plan.

As the train pulled into the next little town, we scanned the streets through the window, looking for a car rental sign. Avis! We grabbed our luggage off the overhead rack and leaped off the train. We rented a car, retrieved the purse, and continued driving to Paris. We did miss our flight, but as travel agents, we learned a tremendous amount. We learned how to navigate Charles DeGaulle airport, how to check in a rental car, what to do if you miss a flight, and we discovered a great airport hotel that is inexpensive and close enough to Paris to take the train into town for dinner and return for the night.

So this is one of our mottos: If something is broken, it only means there's something to be fixed. A problem is nobody's fault, it's only a challenge to meet. That's how we've built our business, and that's how we've built our tours. We've seen how taking women traveling has changed their lives. That heady feeling of "I'm wonderful and anything is possible" happens when you're walking down the streets of Paris. And when you see how other people live, you realize that there really isn't a *right* way.

We haven't had any mentors in creating this business, no blueprints, no business plan. If we had waited until we had loads of confidence, tons of potential and consistently high self-esteem, we would never have started. You can't wait until all your ducks are in a row, because they never will be. You just have to step off the curb and do it. Life is a Wild Woman Adventure!

SYLVIA WARREN

Warren International
Oakland, California

The journey Sylvia Warren undertook in launching Warren International

afforded her the precise experience she needed to become a consultant for

small and mid-sized companies at critical junctures in their development.

Leveraging her success, she has now formed SWOT® Team Consulting

with a business partner, Otis Turner. In response to corporate downsizing,

defense industry cutbacks, and military base closures, Ms. Warren also

assists entrepreneurs in preparing for the transition to business start-up

and operation through an intensive eight-week training program in busi-

ness plan development.

M y entrepreneurial journey accelerated the Sunday after Thanksgiving in 1986 when I had a dream that clarified my pathway. Although my recollection of the details of that dream remain vague to this day, it carried such visceral power that I woke from it with a sense of certainty and heard clearly in my mind the words, "I am finished." I knew that statement referred to the job I was in at the time. Without hesitation, I wrote out my resignation from the company where I had worked for more than fifteen years.

Taking such definitive action based on a dream was certainly not my modus operandi. However, that certainty so permeated every aspect of my being that there was no alternative except to release the security blanket of corporate life.

Without looking back, I was leaving one of the world's leading airlines, the company I had first joined as a flight attendant years before. Motivated by a passion for travel, my planned two-year stint as a stewardess had evolved into ten years as travel benefits during my free time repeatedly took me to incredible destinations in Africa, Europe, Mexico, Canada, Asia, and the Caribbean. However, even the joy of travel could not mask my need for more challenging and rewarding work. That need compelled me to enroll in an MBA program, and later to accept a promotion to the position of account executive in the air freight division.

Working to capture business from Fortune 500, mid-sized, and small companies, I discovered that what I enjoyed in my new position was clarifying clients' needs, providing solutions, and delivering "real" service. My approach proved successful, and this arena honed my consulting abilities. As a result, I expanded my focus in the MBA program. By the time I graduated, I was running two part-time ventures: Warren International, which started as an import and direct sales business; and High Touch-High Tech, a service to train professionals in how to overcome their fear of technology and develop comfort in using personal computers. After my dream, which essentially heralded the completion of my life as an employee, I decided I would transform Warren International into a marketing consulting company targeting small businesses.

My sudden resignation struck the air freight division like a lightning bolt. Managers and co-workers could make no sense of my departure. Why, they wondered, would I voluntarily leave a position as a regional sales manager when I had consistently demonstrated my ability to generate high levels of revenue, had received national and local awards, and achieved considerable recognition for my professional achievements. I received a call from the senior executive vice president who headed the entire freight division. "So you're jumping ship, huh?" he remarked. I calmly replied, "I'm not jumping ship. I'm just headed in the direction of a better opportunity."

In reality, I was not entirely clear about how best to steer my course. Although I had a few clients in the wings, there were no signed contracts. Nevertheless, I felt propelled forward by the visceral power of the dream and force of certainty it imparted.

I developed a rudimentary business plan, identifying potential clients and strategies for reaching them. However, I clearly did not address the subject at the level of detail I now advise for my clients. Without realizing it, I was basically operating on instinct. Frequenting places and events where I could meet other business people and potential clients, I secured my early contracts with small businesses that wanted to grow their customers and revenue. They formed an eclectic and rather random mix of clients, which I found fascinating and exciting. I was on an accelerated learning curve, discovering how diverse types of small businesses worked—or didn't. Warren International was gaining legs in the marketplace.

Then in the late 1980s and early '90s, the recession hit full force. In California economic conditions were more akin to a depression than a recession. My business was barely two years old, and I was unprepared to weather the economic downturn. While I had always managed money well, I began having cash flow problems. This new, utterly disconcerting experience was frightening. As revenues declined, and my inability to reverse the financial setback increased, my situation looked and felt like personal failure, which was excruciatingly painful. In the throes of the crisis, my perspective eroded further. I did not realize how normal it is for any business to go through such cycles, particularly in the midst of adverse market conditions.

My self-esteem matched my financial decline. Forced to contact my family for financial assistance, I reluctantly made the call. I had relished the financial independence I first gained in college, and it was extremely difficult to ask my parents for money. I felt embarrassed, ashamed, and deeply sorrowful that their skepticism about the success of my entrepreneurial venture was perhaps warranted.

As difficulties continued, I considered 9 to 5 employment and sent my resume to prospective employers. However, when offered a job in which the pay was adequate but the work didn't allow me to utilize my professional talent and ability, I was unable to accept it. That same internal mechanism which had catapulted me into business based on a profound dream experience would simply not allow me to detour from my intended entrepreneurial path.

In spite of all the obstacles, Warren International has survived and thrived. When I look back on that time, I realize that experiencing the seemingly overwhelming challenges and making mistakes left me richer than any immediate success could have. The fact that my business didn't automatically work caused me to look inside myself and restructure how I functioned in the world. I released aspects of myself that no longer worked. I changed my life and my perspective about both business and life. I learned that my Lone Ranger attitude was unnatural, and that the natural ecology of any relationship, including business, is interdependence. Without having had to rely on others in the most challenging of circumstances, I probably would not have learned that potent lesson. As the economy moved forward, so did my business. And I emerged at the end of the tunnel with a light that I didn't have access to when I entered.

Now my consulting business facilitates transition for businesses needing or ready to move to the next level of performance and revenue. Business people come to me when their companies are encountering serious difficulty, or when they need assistance in strategically growing their businesses. Working with them, I witness the quality of compassion which has blossomed in me due to the challenges I have faced myself. I continue to be surprised when, by about the third or fourth session, clients begin shifting their perspective, which enables them to make better business decisions. When I ask about their change in mind set, they consistently respond that the way I listen to them allows them to speak candidly about their businesses without feeling judged. As a consequence, they feel free to take a fresh look at themselves, hear themselves, be honest and real. As they clarify critical issues in this way, they reset their intentions, and their businesses take off.

I have been on an entrepreneurial journey that has enhanced who I am and how I function in the world. Now as I walk the high ground, surveying the plateaus behind and before me, I understand how other entrepreneurs can benefit from the depth and richness of my experience without having to endure the same struggle. When I witness business owners build their businesses beyond what they could even conceive, I know that my hard-earned experience is benefiting another entrepreneur.

ROSEMARY GLADSTAR

Sage Mountain Retreat Center
E. Barre, Vermont

The gentle and soft-spoken strength of Rosemary Gladstar has initiated a major revival in the use of medicinal herbs, nationally and internationally, and has built a small empire of thriving businesses. Over the past 25 years, her love of herbs has given rise to a retail store, several different mail order businesses, the Frontier Herb Cooperative natural herbal product line, Traditional Medicinals herbal tea blends, the California School of Herbal Studies, conferences, books, and a retreat center and native plant preserve on 500 acres in Vermont. "My biggest challenge," she says, "has been in the inner battle between maintaining the quiet and ordinary life I love and living in the whirlwind of activity that comes from liking to see things get done."

Sometimes I think my businesses became successful in spite of themselves—and in spite of me. I never had a bank account and didn't even know how to write a check when I opened Rosemary's Garden, my first herb store, in 1971. I ran it for nine years without even having a bookkeeping system! I wouldn't necessarily recommend that method—eventually all the businesses had to grow up. But even at the point when I had to make them work well, it wasn't with the idea that I was going to run several really successful businesses. I never thought in those terms. I just was doing things I loved and found exciting.

Even though I thought small in terms of business, my vision has been really big—to bring healing herbs back into use—whether that meant providing herbal remedies for my friends and neighbors in the early seventies or holding international conferences of herbalists in the nineties.

Ever since I was a small child, my major love has been the plants. My earliest teachings were from my grandmother who lived with us when I was growing up. For a couple of years after high school, I backpacked through wild areas of the Pacific Northwest and lived in tiny remote cabins. That's where I honed my herbal skills. I consider that time my college education—being with the plants and learning from them.

In 1970, I returned home to Sonoma County in northern California, with a baby and a dream of buying horses and riding the Pacific Crest trail. To earn money for that, I got a job as a cleaning lady in a little health food store. Within a couple of months, the owner of the store recognized that I knew quite a bit about herbs and hired me to run their small herb section. That was the beginning of Traditional Medicinals which was started as a cooperative venture by myself and two close friends. At the time we didn't think of it as the start of a major business—we were simply formulating teas for local people to help them get well or stay healthy. As they came back and told us how the formulas worked for them, we changed and refined them.

The next spring I got my horses and, with a girlfriend and my two-year-old son, set out. We took no food with us and for four-and-a-half months lived entirely off wild plants. It is one of the most outstanding things I have ever done. I felt as if I were being given many gifts from the plants during that journey, and that was when I made a real commitment to work with herbs. We rode as far into the Trinity Alps as we could, then returned to Sonoma County in the fall.

I bought the herb section of the natural food store, rented a little room in back about the size of a closet, and opened Rosemary's Garden. The purpose of the store was simply to provide herbal remedies for my community, like a home-dispensary. I just thought, "These people need a place to get herbs, and I love herbs, so I'll just get some together for them." My thinking never went beyond that.

When people who knew me wanted to learn more about herbs, I started teaching my first herb class. I'm the first to admit that when I started teaching, I probably knew less than almost anybody today who is involved with herbs. Twenty-five years ago very little was known about herbal healing or how to make tinctures or salves. The Herb Society of America, one of the few herbal organizations at the time, dealt strictly with gardening and culinary herbs; medicinals were not at all popular.

With a small group of herbalists in 1974, I held what I believe was the first conference on medicinal herbs in the country. We handwrote flyers and posted them around locally. We charged $25 for the weekend, including food and lodging. Fifty people came to that first gathering, and we had four teachers all of whom went on to become nationally known herbalists. Within a few years those retreats grew from 50 to 500 and more, and they still continue all over the country.

Each step happened so organically. People taking classes started wanting more and deeper information. Looking back, I think we were actually creating the need to know more. When I realized that so many people wanted to study herbalism in depth, I started the California School of Herbal Studies. We brought in other teachers, had beautiful herb gardens, and a community of people lived there, running it and teaching.

During that time Rosemary's Garden had grown, moved to a new location, and had also become a mail order business. I was teaching at retreats and at the herb school, and raising my son and stepchildren. I think at each step if I had paused to think what I was doing, I would have been frightened of the massive responsibility and probably not have continued. But one of my failures—or one of my greatest gifts—is not to see problems, and that has kept me moving. I wasn't a prime candidate for operating businesses, but I did have gifts that allowed me to carry out a vision.

Until my children were in early adolescence, we lived simply, without electricity, close to the land. As they grew and the businesses grew, I realized that even though I was running all these businesses, we were still poor. I thought, "I don't mind living like a pauper, but I feel I shouldn't have to work so hard to do it! If I work this hard, there's got to be a return. And if we don't do something about pulling these businesses together, they won't be happening anymore." It was one more challenge—and I was ready for it!

I knew where all the leaky holes in the bucket were. That didn't take much business sense. I had a sloppy budget without any defined goals as to what was going into advertising, payroll, retreats, etc. I had too many work exchange students in classes and on retreats. These were the kind of things I should have thought of on Day One, but that isn't how I've done anything. I don't regret it, because everything has worked very beautifully for me. I might have if the businesses had failed. But after a couple of years of resisting the inevitable, I knew I had to take the reins into my hands and focus on the business aspect of all these endeavors. I had to learn how to be a good organizer.

The very fact that I hadn't seen myself as an entrepreneur also meant that I didn't look at challenges that came up in the businesses as setbacks or hindrances. I figured they were just aspects of being involved in something bigger than any of us as individuals. The many people who've been part of this vision and this dream have brought their weaknesses, their problems, their ill health, and also their talents and the gift of the beautiful beings they are. That is what has made herbalism come back into our world.

Along the way, I have turned businesses over to others. My early partner in Traditional Medicinals, Drake Sadler, took over the business part, and I went into the educational part; I really didn't want to be in manufacturing and have to put my skills into how many bottles and how many ounces. I sold Rosemary's Garden and leased the formulas for the product line. Two of my students were interested in the mail order part of that business, and I sold it to them for the small sum of $3000! Because they didn't have the money to buy the formulas, I leased them to them with a renewable lease every six years. When I moved to Vermont, my two step-daughters and I started a family business that they ran to help pay for their college education. That's a mail order business called Sage Mountain Herbs—which is quite successful!

I am the most unconventional business person. But I have enough money from what I do. One of the things I have realized as I earn more—because all of these businesses do very well financially—is that I am faced with the challenge of moderating my success. I was planning to double the size of my facilities so I could have bigger classes and do more programs, and then I realized that was absolutely not what I wanted to do. Why would I need to do that? First, it's better for the students when classes are small, and second, I don't need more money. What would I do with it? Buy more, invest more?

I also made a firm commitment not to create any more products. The world doesn't need any more good herbal products. There's enough out there. There's enough marketing, there's enough competition, there's just enough. The most important thing right now for many people is not making more or doing more or trying to create more; it's finding more time just to live.

I've devoted my entire life to bringing herbalism back, to making it a people's healing art, to getting people to develop their own formulas and start ethical companies. For 25 years I have been watching what has been happening as more people have started using herbs and started herb businesses. One day I stepped back and said, "Look at all the resources it has used up." In this country many of our major medicinal herbs are considered either endangered or threatened. I feel like part of the problem. As an herbalist my primary concern should be caring for the earth and the plants that come from it, not using them up.

So I have started what I hope is my last major project, a nonprofit organization called United Plant Savers, which has nothing to do with business. It is the biggest endeavor I have ever undertaken as far as my level of commitment and the implications of the project. Its sole purpose is to restore and replant endangered medicinal species, and it is getting a tremendous response.

All along, my vision was not to run a business but to preserve an herbal tradition. That was the vision I had years ago at a time when our minds were clear and beautiful and potent. Why my businesses have worked so well is that they were all serving that bigger vision. I think when we find something that empowers or impassions us, and we are willing to work hard at it, it will succeed. Sometimes I sit back and laugh, because doing this work is as enchanting now as it was the day when I opened my first herb store.

ELLEN TERRY

Ellen Terry, Realtors
Dallas, Texas

After fifteen years as owner and President of Ellen Terry, Realtors, Dallas's premier Boutique specialty firm, Ellen Terry sold her multi-million dollar firm to her hero and mentor, Ebby Halliday. Ms. Halliday is the founder of a 50-year-old firm which is the largest independently owned residential real estate company in Texas. Ellen Terry, Realtors is also the exclusive Dallas affiliate for Sotheby International Realty and the Estates Club, both known for marketing prestige properties. With a strong dedication to community service, Ellen Terry's efforts have substantially benefited local charities. She is an inspiring motivational speaker and is in the process of writing a book on her personal and business philosophy.

Whehen people achieve success in life, we often see and hear only the good parts. It can appear as if it was very easy for them or that they became successful because they were born with a silver spoon in their mouth. But most successful people have faced failure, pain and many setbacks before achieving the gain. What makes most people successful is the never-giving-up and the continual coming back for one more round each time they get knocked down. They have learned to reject the rejections in life.

In 1976 at the age of 37, I had to come face to face with a total life change. I was a carefree Dallas housewife who thought she had the world on a string. My balloon was filled with affluence, security, family, leisure, a home in a prestigious area of Dallas, a Mercedes, expensive clothes and jewelry. I spent my time shopping at Neiman Marcus, working on charity events, volunteering for the Junior League, and playing tennis with my friends. I was living the American dream insulated by my protective bubble of the "right groups" and the "right people." I felt immune to disaster.

Suddenly and without warning my balloon burst. I was hosting a Junior League meeting in my home when the doorbell rang. Assuming it was a late-arriving member, I went to the door with a smile on my face. There stood a man in mechanic's overalls. "Is Ms. Terry here?" he asked. "I'm Ms. Terry," I said, still not suspecting anything. "Well, I'm here to pick up the keys to your Mercedes. The payments haven't been made in a number of months."

The blood raced from the top of my head to the bottom of my toes. I did have the sanity to walk out on my front porch and pull the door closed so that the Junior League was not privy to what was taking place. I said, "This can't be true. You've got to be mistaken." I looked out and saw the tow truck. My first thought was, "This man is nuts. The Junior League is in my living room, and he doesn't even know it." When you're a member of the Junior League, these things don't happen to you. But I found out, they in fact do happen. Reality was staring me in the face.

The financial disaster I was about to encounter was far worse than I could have ever imagined. Within a few months, I discovered that because Texas is a community property state, I was in debt to the IRS for over $100,000. I had never balanced a checkbook or bothered to check the bank or savings account. I had never dealt with a banker, CPA, or an attorney. I had grown up living the Cinderella/Prince Charming story—the house with the white picket fence, the two perfect children, and the lifestyle of happily-ever-after. I grew up believing that the wife would be taken care of by the husband. I've learned that all of us as individuals must be accountable and responsible for our own lives, whether we are male or female. Two major mistakes I made during the eleven years of my marriage were my ignorance about our financial situation and lack of any definitive personal goals for my life. I was floating along, oblivious to my circumstances. When disaster hit, I wanted to put my head in the sand like an ostrich and pretend it would all go away. It didn't.

I've come to believe that everything that happens in life has a purpose and that each circumstance can turn from a challenging opportunity into positive personal growth. I had been taught by my parents to believe in myself, to have strong self-esteem, to have faith in a Supreme Being, and no matter what the circumstances were, to be a fighter, not a quitter. This was my chance to be tested by fire.

I sold my clothing, jewelry, and furniture to pay creditors, moved into a one-bedroom efficiency apartment and went to work for a friend at a travel agency. The hardest part of all was sending my children to live with their grandparents for seven months. My daughter was six years old and my son was eight. I couldn't afford to pay for after-school care while I worked, and I knew their grandparents could give them the nurturing and stable environment they needed while I was trying to get my feet on the ground financially. There is no way to explain the feelings I endured when I delivered them to their grandparents. It was excruciatingly painful even though I knew it was the right thing to do.

I soon realized that working at a travel agency wasn't going to afford me the resources as a single parent to bring my children back home with me and provide them with the things I felt they needed. After interviewing with several companies, I decided that selling real estate was what I most wanted to do. It would have flexible hours, so that I could pick up my children from school, go to my son's soccer games, and take my daughter to ballet classes. I went to real estate school on the weekends and took a cram course to learn the math for the real estate exam.

Then one morning, a few days after the exam, I was driving to my job at the travel agency in the 1967 army green Oldsmobile my mother had loaned me after my car was repossessed. I was waiting at a stop light and happened to glance over to my right. There next to me in her 500SEL Mercedes was one of my former students from the exclusive girls' school where I had taught prior to getting married. I hoped she wouldn't see me in my ugly, ten-year-old, non-descript car . . . but she did and motioned for me to open my window. I leaned over and rolled down the window. I told her I was getting my real estate license and asked if she knew of anyone looking for a house. "We may be," she said. "Call me." The light changed, I rolled up the window, put my hands on the wheel, and prayed that I had passed the math on the real estate exam.

I did pass, and my real estate career began with a national company that had just opened in Dallas. They told me that it might take six to nine months to make my first sale. I convinced them that, if that was the case, I must have a draw against future commissions or I couldn't go into real estate. They agreed to a $500 a month draw for six months. On my first day in the office, I worked up the courage and called my former student. "Are you serious about looking for a house?" I asked. "Yes." she said, "but we don't want to spend a penny over $400,000." I tried to contain my excitement and said, "Oh, I'll see if we have something that inexpensive in our inventory." Within 30 days I had sold my first house. Within 45 days, I had sold my second house and earned over $12,000, which was more money than I had earned in a year working at the travel agency. I had the honor of being recognized as Coldwell Banker's Number One sales associate in the state of Texas and Number Two in the nation for two straight years. The same month I sold my first two houses, I brought my children back home to live with me. The next two years were spent in a very successful partnership with two other women, creating a Boutique residential real estate company with 35 agents.

In 1981 I decided to start my own Boutique company, specializing in the high-end market of buying and selling million dollar properties. I found that I loved inspiring and motivating others to become the very best in the business. Being the sole owner and managing my own company was a new and exciting challenge for me. The first five years, Ellen Terry, Realtors was phenomenally successful. In 1985 our sales volume with fewer than fifty agents was over $180 million. Each success led to a desire for more.

I was working round the clock. My children were home with a babysitter, and although I worried about not spending a lot of time with them, I had become completely obsessed with my company and the desire to bring home a lot of money in order to provide my children with what I thought they needed and wanted. When the economy in Texas took an absolute nosedive in 1986, our sales plunged with it. I thought I had encountered the worst with these challenges, only to find that my son had become addicted to drugs and alcohol and needed to enter a treatment center. Once again I found myself facing a sobering reality—making money and building a successful company didn't preclude me from experiencing excruciating pain.

As devastating as this situation was, it was the beginning of a wonderful recovery process for our entire family. Attending the weekly family seminars with my son, my own eyes were opened to the fact that not only did he have an addiction to drugs and alcohol, I too had a major addiction to work and the adrenaline high of creating more and more success. The only difference was that my addiction got applauded by society while his was shamed. I realized that I had been working to provide for material things, and what my children needed most from me was for me to be there for them physically and emotionally.

I continued to work hard, but I shifted my focus more towards my children. My family has continued to work toward recovery, the economy in Texas slowly recovered; and my business, despite a lot of struggle, built back our high volume of sales. The pain once again created gain. Wanting to share what I had learned, I created an Awareness Hour for parents, students and teachers at the local high school, bringing in well-known speakers in the field of substance abuse. I strongly believe that companies have an obligation to give back to the community that supports them and to reach out and make a difference in the lives of others.

Upon turning 50, I determined that the second half of my life was going to be lived with more balance. I set a goal that I would sell Ellen Terry, Realtors within five years. A few months before my 55th birthday, I called the woman who has been my mentor and inspiration since I started my own company. Ebby Halliday, the Grande Dame of Dallas residential real estate, had built her company on the highest standards of honesty, integrity, professionalism and fairness to all clients and customers. These are the very same principles I valued when founding Ellen Terry, Realtors.

Just before my 56th birthday, Ebby bought the company. I had met my goal. We agreed that I would continue working for the company, doing what I love the most—selling and listing high-end properties and no longer having to manage the office. There has definitely been some grief and adjustment in giving up the role of boss; however, the joy has far outweighed the pain. I have come full circle and am back to the basics.

When I look back, one of the things I would do differently is spend more quality time with my children. But I'm not sure I had that option at the time. I think we just do the best we can with what we have and what we know. Life's best lessons are derived from the challenging opportunities; viewing them with hindsight, we develop wisdom.

Each of us is a precious child of God, put here for a special and unique purpose, a spiritual being having a human experience. To me, this is the essence of what life is all about. When we come up against challenges—and owning a business is certain to bring them—we begin to mature and grow into who God truly intended us to become—Human Beings rather than Human Doings.

CONTACTS FOR WOMEN
BUSINESS OWNERS FEATURED

Raydean Acevedo
Research Management
    Consultants, Inc. (RMCI)
1746 Cole Boulevard
Bldg. 2, Suite 300
Golden, CO 80401
(303) 277-0066

Barbara Beckmann
Barbara Beckmann Designs, Inc.
2425 - 17th Street
San Francisco, CA 94110
(415) 863-6982

Laurel Burch
Laurel Burch Gallerie
539 Bridgeway
Sausalito, CA 94965
(415) 332-7764

Kristi Cowles
Pederson Victorian
    Bed & Breakfast
Singing Wolf Center
1782 Highway 120 North
Lake Geneva, WI 53147
(414) 248-9110

Susan Davis
Capital Missions Company
31W007 North Avenue,
Suite 101
West Chicago, IL 60185
(708) 876-1101

Eileen Tabata Fitzpatrick
Kanojo
18003 Sky Park Circle, #G
Irvine, CA 92714
(714) 955-2250

Sr. Rosalind Gefre
Professional Massage Center
2221 Ford Parkway, Suite 200
St. Paul, MN 55116-1800
(612) 698-9123

Rosemary Gladstar
Sage Mountain
P.O. Box 420
E. Barre, VT 05649
(802) 479-9825

Belinda Guadarrama
GC Micro Corporation
6100 Redwood Blvd.
Novato, CA 94945

Patrice Harrison-Inglis
Sweetwoods Dairy
P.O. Box 1238
Pena Blanca, NM 87041
(505) 465-2608

Polly Helm
Pendleton Cowgirl Co., Inc.
P.O. Box 19474
Portland, OR 97280-0474
(503) 977-0292
www.cowgirlcompany.com
e-mail:
Polly@cowgirlcompany.com

Sarahn Henderson
Mother's Keeper
8333 Glenwoods Drive
Riverdale, GA 30274
(770) 473-1473

Theresa Martinez Hoffacker
Constant Care Day School
#3 Dovela Place
Santa Fe, NM 87505
(505) 466-4629

Barbara Hughley
Media Professionals, Inc.
1830 Grand Avenue, Suite C
Baldwin, NY 11510
(516) 867-1000

Marjorie Kelly
Business Ethics
P.O. Box 8439
Minneapolis, MN 55408
(612) 879-0695

Jenai Lane
Respect
300 Brannan Street #603
San Francisco, CA 94107
(415) 512-8997

Susan Levy
Femi-9 Contracting Corporation
305 East Sunrise Highway
Lindenhurst, NY 11757
(516) 884-3656

Martha Lindt & Carol Rivendell
Wild Women Adventures
107 N. Main Street
Sebastopol, CA 95472
(707) 829-3670

Nabila Mango
Mango Trading Services
311 41st Avenue
San Mateo, CA 94403
(415) 341-3697

Carolyna Marks
World Wall for Peace
1427 Milvia Street
Berkeley, CA 94709
(510) 527-2356

Gayle McEnroe
Metal Service Inc.
312 Walnut Street
St. Paul, MN 55102
(612) 222-8623

Assunta Ng
Seattle Chinese Post
Northwest Asian Weekly
414 8th Avenue S.
P.O. Box 3468
Seattle, WA 98104
(206) 223-0623

Ann Ruethling
Chinaberry Books
2780 Via Orange Way #B
Spring Valley, CA 91978

Tami Simon
Sounds True Catalog
P.O. Box 8010
Boulder, CO 80306-8010
(303) 665-3151

Ellen Terry
Ellen Terry, Realtors
5401 North Central Expressway,
  #225
Dallas, TX 75205
(214) 522-3838

Sylvia Warren
Warren International
SWOT® TEAM
  CONSULTING
1856 Franklin Street, Suite 5
San Francisco, CA 94109
(415) 673-1216

Lynn Winter
Lynn's Paradise Cafe
984 Barret Avenue
Louisville, KY 40204
(502) 583-EGGS

Patrice Wynne
GAIA Bookstore and Community
  Center
1400 Shattuck Avenue
Berkeley, CA 94709
(510) 548-4172 (Store)
(510) 548-4178 (Office)

Books by The Crossing Press

No More Frogs, No More Princes: Women Making Creative Choices in Midlife
Interviews by Joanne Vickers and Barbara Thomas
This book contains 20 women's stories by typical American women who woke up to the possibilities of midlife creativity and met life head on.
$10.95 • Paper • ISBN 0-89594-625-4

On Women Turning Forty: Coming Into Our Fullness
By Cathleen Rountree
These candid interviews and beautiful photographs will inspire all women who are navigating through the midlife passage. The updated look of this bestselling classic makes it the perfect companion to the later decades of Rountree's series on women.
16.00 • Paper • ISBN 0-89594-517-7

Writing from the Heart: Inspiration and Exercises for Women Who Want to Write
By Lesléa Newman
"There's more to this book than inspiration. For presenting the basics of writing structure and technique, this book has few peers."
—*Lambda Book Report*
$12.95 • Paper • ISBN 0-89594-641-6

Pocket Guide to Visualization
By Helen Graham
$6.95 • Paper • ISBN 0-89594-885-0

To receive a current catalog from The Crossing Press, please call toll-free, 800-777-1048.
Visit our Website on the Internet at: www.crossingpress.com